william krisel's palm springs

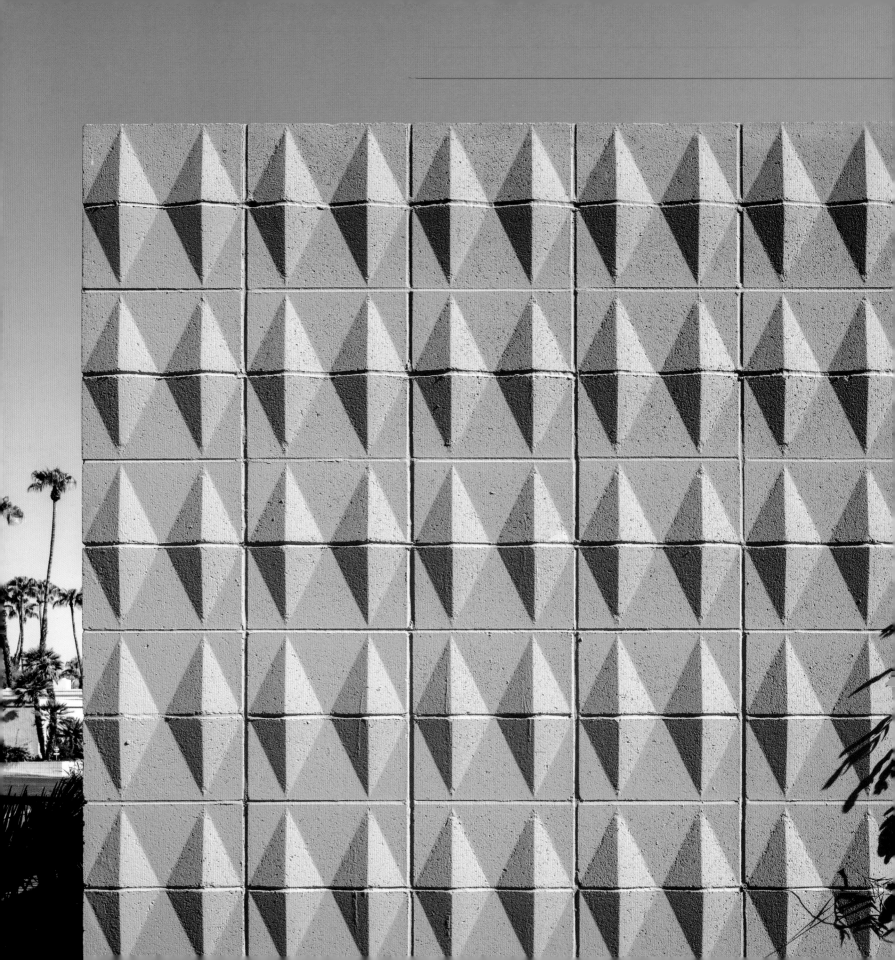

william krisel's palm springs

THE LANGUAGE OF MODERNISM

edited by CHRIS MENRAD and HEIDI CREIGHTON

GIBBS SMITH
TO ENRICH AND INSPIRE HUMANKIND

First Edition
24 23 22   10 9

Published by
Gibbs Smith
P.O. Box 667
Layton, Utah 84041

1.800.835.4993 orders
www.gibbs-smith.com

Designed by Gary Wexler
Photo restoration and retouch by Darren Bradley

Printed and bound in China

Gibbs Smith books are printed on either recycled,
100% post-consumer waste, FSC-certified papers
or on paper produced from sustainable PEFC-certified
forest/controlled wood source. Learn more at www.pefc.org.

Library of Congress Cataloging-in-Publication Data

Names: Menrad, Chris, editor. | Creighton, Heidi, editor. | Krisel,
William, 1924- Works. Selections.
Title: William Krisel's Palm Springs : the language of modernism / edited
by Chris Menrad and Heidi Creighton.
Description: First Edition. | Layton, Utah : Gibbs Smith, 2016. |
Includes index.
Identifiers: LCCN 2015032682 | ISBN 9781423642329
Subjects: LCSH: Krisel, William, 1924—Criticism and interpretation. |
Midcentury modern (Architecture)   California   Palm Springs. |
Architect-designed houses—California—Palm Springs—History—20th
century. | Palm Springs (Calif.)—Buildings, structures, etc.
Classification: LCC NA737.K75 W55 2016 | DDC 720.92—dc23
LC record available at http://lccn.loc.gov/2015032682

Previous overleaf: Detail of shadow block wall,
Sandpiper, Palm Desert, California (2015).
Photograph © Darren Bradley.

Perhaps more than any other architect, Bill Krisel is responsible for Palm Springs' renown as an international mecca for Midcentury Modern house design. With an astute understanding of how to build in the desert, Krisel brought elegant design to multifamily housing, building tens of thousands of affordable units. His sublime single-family residences with their "butterfly" roofs are iconic symbols of contemporary Palm Springs living, capturing the spirit of the desert and its exuberant lifestyle. —**STEVEN EHRLICH, FAIA**

Bill Krisel's masterful hand and ideals were a perfect recipe for the development of Modernism in Southern California, particularly in the desert cities. Based on the tenet that good, thoughtful design should be for everyone, Bill's legacy must be seen as purely democratic. His work, although nicely fitting into the scene of the time and the place, was original and authentic. This was architecture that was void of hyperbole, sensationalism, formalism, and falsehood. It is even stronger today and strengthens over time, half a century later. His incessant energy and optimism produced mountains of work that has its tentacles far reaching, influencing architecture for generations to come. —**ZOLTAN PALI, FAIA**

I cannot remember my first meetings with the Krisels, as I was too small. But while growing up, they were a constant presence in my family life. Indeed, when I was old enough, I was a babysitter for their young children. My dad spoke very highly of both Bill and Corinne. Of course my father's [architect Paul Laszlo] relationship with Bill was both professional and personal. Bill worked with my dad when he was starting out, and I've always believed that my dad considered himself a mentor to Bill. I know that Bill was influenced by my dad's designs and my dad liked Bill's work very much. Indeed, at age seventy-six, my father bought a condominium in one of Bill's large condominium projects in Santa Monica, where he lived seventeen years. A great tribute, I believe. —**PETER LASZLO**

The critical premise proposed by Krisel that solidified the development and helped define the architecture of Palm Springs was in convincing the Alexanders that these homes had to be different than those in the city [Los Angeles]. Unlike the city, these were second homes and vacation destinations geared towards "the guy who wanted to trade in his three-piece suit and four-door car for walking shorts, golf bag, and a seat by the pool." With such an appeal, the projects privileged an open plan and indoor/outdoor spatial experience enabled by post-and-beam construction, tailored to a lifestyle of entertainment and leisure. —**ALVIN HUANG, AIA**

I AM NOT A modern ARCHITECT.

"Modern" MEANS ONLY "OF THE CURRENT TIME." IT IMPLIES A PRESENT STYLE WHICH
COULD EASILY BE OUTMODED TOMORROW. INSTEAD I AM AN ARCHITECT WHO BELIEVES
IN modernism, WHICH IS A PHILOSOPHY, A LANGUAGE, A FUNDAMENTAL BELIEF, AN
"ISM" JUST LIKE LIBERALISM, CONSERVATISM, CAPITALISM, SOCIALISM, ETC.

Modernism IS A PHILOSOPHY THAT CREATES A BETTER WAY OF LIVING THROUGH DESIGN. IT
IMPROVES ONE'S APPRECIATION OF DESIGN AND ECOLOGY.

Modernism IS NOT A STYLE. IT IS NOT STATIC. IT IS LIKE FRENCH, ENGLISH, RUSSIAN,
CHINESE OR ANY LANGUAGE: THE BASIC VOCABULARY—THE WORDS—REMAIN THE
SAME OVER TIME, BUT IT ADAPTS TO NEW CONDITIONS AND NEW TECHNOLOGY. IT ADDS
NEW WORDS, AND ENFOLDS THEM INTO THE ONGOING LANGUAGE.

MY LANGUAGE OF modernism IS THE SAME TODAY AS IT WAS IN THE 1950S. IT HAS
ADDED THE NEW WORDS, THE NEW TECHNOLOGIES, THAT HAVE COME INTO
EXISTENCE AND CHANGED OUR LIVES.

THE DIFFERENCE BETWEEN THE MEANING OF "modern" AS A STYLE AND "modernism" AS
A PHILOSOPHY IS CRUCIAL TO UNDERSTANDING WHAT I DO—AND WHAT I WON'T DO—IN
ARCHITECTURE, LANDSCAPE DESIGN, AND PLANNING.

William Krisel, A.I.A.

Facing: Mike Lee and Deborah Rumens
Residence (formerly the Dunas Residence),
Palm Springs, California (2015).

Photograph © Darren Bradley.

contents

Tract house with flat roof
in Racquet Club Estates,
Palm Springs, California (2015).

Photograph © Darren Bradley.

Rendering of

Kemp Residence,

Palm Desert, California

(undated)—detail.[1]

KEMP RESIDENCE

foreword

WIM DE WIT

Adjunct Curator of Architecture and Design, Cantor Arts Center, Stanford University

During my twenty-plus years as curator of architecture and design at the Getty Research Institute in Los Angeles, I have acquired countless archives of architects and other kinds of designers. In general, I still remember the contents of all these collections, but I cannot always recall anymore how I first heard about them or when I first saw them. This is not a problem I have with the William Krisel papers. I remember distinctly that Bill and his wife, Corinne, approached me after a public lecture at the Getty Center and asked me if they could have a meeting with me. Aware of who they were, I agreed. Our first meeting started out on neutral territory somewhere in the L.A. area. Bill had many questions about what the Getty's registrars and catalogers do with the various kinds of materials that one can find in an archive. They were the typical kinds of questions from someone who has taken care of his papers for decades and who now wants to pass on those materials to someone who will take just as good care of them. After that discussion we went to the Krisel house (now unfortunately destroyed) on Tigertail Road in Brentwood, where part of the archive was stored in flat-file drawers. Here Bill's approach was very to the point. Like a good businessman, he knew how to sell his work to me and immediately showed me the best part of the archive: his large-sized renderings, primarily in graphite, on large sheets of white vellum.

This was a very good move. I have visited with other owners of archives who, in order to test you, present the archive to you piecemeal to see how you respond to each document and thus to find out if you are the right curator for the archive. There is of course nothing wrong with such an approach, but Bill's method was quite the opposite and very effectual. He proudly presented a batch of spectacular drawings: perspectival representations of many of his

projects (houses, apartment buildings, medical offices, and storefronts) perfectly laid out on the page, rendered with intense contrasts between light and dark, and almost always animated by large 1950s or '60s cars and his famous twin palm trees. Bill's tactic of "selling" the archive to me worked. I knew pretty quickly that I wanted to acquire this archive, but had to ask anyway what else there was in addition to these renderings. When I was told that there were also working drawings, papers, photographs, and slides, I knew that this was an archive that I had to add to the Getty's growing collection of archives documenting Southern California architecture.

Amidst all those archives at the Getty, Krisel's drawings stand out because of their display of confidence. I have often in my mind compared Krisel's drawings to those of his contemporaries. The drawings of Pierre Koenig, for example, almost always show a struggle—a struggle about the question of how to make the perfect house out of steel and glass. In each design, Koenig attempted over and over to create a house that both structurally and in detail was going to be better than his previous ones. He often managed to outperform himself, but his drawings show that those successes did not come easily to him. There is a certain hesitation in the lines that make up his drawings, and only

rarely does one have the feeling that Koenig enjoyed the aesthetics of laying out the various pieces of the drawing on the sheet of paper. Krisel's drawings, on the other hand, show a total joy of producing the drawing. Even when he was designing a project of dozens of more or less the same tract houses, he was able to express a feeling of excitement through his drawings. He achieved that quality through the use of some very interesting drafting techniques. His drawings are often worm's-eye views, which means that one looks up at the building from below. The viewer's eye is more or less at the level of the lawn or the pavement of the street. That perspective gives the observer the feeling that

the structure is not trying to hide from view and instead presents itself majestically. These drawings always remind me a little bit of the famous sketch drawings by German architect Erich Mendelsohn (1887–1953), but without the prominent arc of the sky that the latter drew over every building in his perspective views. Mendelsohn and Krisel definitely have in common that they both used shadows to articulate the diverse volumes that make up the total building. Krisel, however, took his shading technique a bit further. Like architects of the seventeenth, eighteenth, and nineteenth centuries, Krisel rendered the windows in his buildings black. Unlike his predecessors, Krisel did not

Rendering of R. Altman
Construction project,
Scottsdale, Arizona
(undated)—detail.

Gift of William and Corinne Krisel.
William Krisel Architectural Archive,
Getty Research Institute,
Los Angeles (2009.M.23).
© J. Paul Getty Trust.

Rendering of casita patio,
Ocotillo Lodge, Palm Springs,
California (circa 1955)—detail.

make his windowpanes solidly black. When one looks carefully, one can see geometric shapes representing the sunlight's projection on the floor or an inside wall. As a result, the rendering becomes more than a representation of the facade. The light adds depth to the rendering, and one realizes that one is looking at a drawing of a real building. And making representations of real buildings was what Krisel was always after in his drawings. While the human figures in his drawings (pretentious-looking men or women with voluptuous hips) may suggest that these renderings were just made for fun, all drawings were made for actual buildings. Depictions of follies or fantasy structures cannot be found in the Krisel archive.

The question that then arises is, why did Bill Krisel make these drawings? One might think that renderings made with so much attention to detail and, especially, with so much contrast between the lights and the shadows were made for publication in one of the architectural magazines of Krisel's time. Publicity, however, was not at all on the architect's mind when he worked on these drawings. He presumably thought that architectural photography, for which he commissioned Julius Shulman, would suffice to do that work. For Krisel, these drawings played a crucial role at an earlier stage in the design process than the one during which a finished house was publicized. In fact, he considered them essential components of that process. In conversations about his work, Krisel gives three reasons for making these drawings. The first one is that he wanted to make certain that the building would indeed work as he had imagined it in the early sketch phase. If there were a problem in the design, these drawings would reveal it to him. Second, the rendering was, of course, a good means to convince the client that this was the right design that should be built. Krisel's third reason is that he liked making them. The work of finishing the drawings (after the initial preparatory

projections had been taken care of) was even used as a distraction: he drew the human figures, the palm trees and other vegetation, the lawns, and the shadows while he was engaged in long telephone conversations with a contractor or developer. Working on the drawings thus gave him the sense that the tedious time spent on these conversations was nonetheless enjoyable.

It is probably this delight in making architecture that homeowners in Los Angeles and Palm Springs have felt over the years and that recently has made Krisel's houses so popular again. Consistently designed in a Midcentury Modern vocabulary, large numbers of these houses have survived the time and are now being restored to their original condition again. And because he had personally drawn or supervised the design of every detail, Krisel remembers almost every building component, and is therefore still able to provide invaluable and cost-saving advice to the new owners.

This volume dedicated to Krisel's work in Palm Springs—a metropolitan area where he has built so many significant structures—will undoubtedly further clarify what made his work so special. And, as almost always happens with publications, films, or exhibitions, it will hopefully generate many new studies in which this book's authors' ideas about Krisel's oeuvre will be further examined, discussed, and disseminated.

NOTES

1. The dates in parentheses refer to the date the image was created. The word "detail" in this caption and others throughout the book refers to images from the Getty Research Institute that have been cropped from their original dimensions.

words from a book instigator

HEIDI CREIGHTON

Backyard view of the
Creighton Residence,
Twin Palms, Palm Springs,
California (2015).

Photograph © Darren Bradley.

While my collaborators have had a longer association with Midcentury Modern architecture and some have forged close personal relationships with William Krisel, I arrived relatively late on the scene.

In 2012, I purchased a William Krisel–designed sun flap home in the Twin Palms neighborhood of Palm Springs—a Model A-3, I was later to learn. It struck me when walking around the neighborhood, at the south end of Palm Springs, that what appealed to me about this house and community had been embedded deep in my psyche over fifty years ago.

I grew up in Don Mills, Ontario, Canada's first planned community. My childhood home was one of over three thousand built upon the basis of planning principles for the new subdivision, never implemented anywhere in Canada before. These principles included separation of pedestrian and vehicle traffic; promotion of Modernist architecture and the modern aesthetic; creation of a greenbelt; and integration of industry into the community.

Of course as a child wandering around in my large (to me) world with my pals in the neighborhood, these principles wouldn't have meant much. But I like to think that my early introduction to living within our version of Modernism not only planted memories but informed my later evolving aesthetic and an appreciation for the particular "language" that Mr. Krisel speaks so eloquently.

These memories would be awakened in the Krisel tract house that was constructed a year after my birth some 2,500 miles and many climatic zones away.

I now wander around in a serious yet lighthearted home. Serious because the house is solid. It has an elegant yet understated presence. It doesn't reveal too much structurally from the street unless you are familiar with Krisel's sun

Sun flap on the west-facing elevation of the Creighton Residence (2015). Krisel recommended the removal of half of the roof material behind the sun flap during restoration in 2012 to allow more light into the interior and shadow play on the exterior.

Photograph © Darren Bradley.

had elected to use modern, desert-friendly materials like stone and cacti, and most surprising to me was the approval of eco-friendly rubber mulch. I had never seen it used in such an expressive way—blue and brown patterns interspersed with lava stones and pebbles. It completely captivated me before I had even set foot inside the house.

Besides restoring my home, Chris Menrad is also a neighbor, living just five doors down from me in a more recognizable butterfly-roof house. We talked from time to time about how often William Krisel is mentioned in books and articles about Midcentury Modern architecture in California, but there were none dedicated to his contribution. We agreed that it was high time a book focusing on Krisel's considerable body of work was written.

Luckily for us, Krisel agreed and we began to put together a collection of excellent collaborators: architects, architectural historians, preservationists, a landscape architect, and landscape photographers—all experts in their fields, activists for Midcentury Modernism, and devoted to Krisel and his work.

I need to commend Chris Menrad, especially for his tireless efforts to educate the rest of us about this important architecture in Palm Springs and his passionate dedication to Krisel and his work in the desert.

As for me, I like to think of myself as a book instigator—a William Krisel book instigator. I can attest that it has been a privileged position.

flap construction or use of patterned concrete block. But once inside this light-infused home, private yet open, I felt reflected in it—that we were a unit of sorts. I suppose this is how one feels when one has arrived "home."

I learned that Mr. Krisel, at the age of eighty-eight, was involved in the restoration of the house with Chris Menrad and J. R. Roberts. Although I hadn't met him yet, Chris and J. R. showed me their updated plans for the home. Two areas were of great interest to me. The first had to do with the sun flaps. Krisel had agreed to open them up to allow for more light. The second more obvious area, at least from the street, was the unique landscaping. Not only had Krisel designed the sweeping curves through the driveway, but he

Finally, I would like to thank Mr. Krisel for the wonderful opportunity to learn more about him and his work, his great patience as I floundered around the subject, and most importantly, I think, his generous and optimistic view of what is possible and what can be done if you work extremely efficiently and with complete devotion as his architecture and landscape design remind me everyday in my sun flap Model A-3 home.

acknowledgments

A house is a muse—a structure that can ignite a conversation about living with great design and the architect who created it. This is what can happen when you live in an Alexander home in Twin Palms Estates in Palm Springs, California, designed by William Krisel. At least this is what happened to us.

While there are books, articles, conferences, and documentary films that have included the work of William Krisel, especially identifying his Midcentury Modern architecture in California, this is the first book that examines his work in the Coachella Valley. In fact, this is the first book that focuses *only* on the work of this important architect.

We have been privileged to collaborate with Mr. Krisel, including discussing his buildings while reviewing material with him at his archives in the Getty Research Institute, and e-mailing questions about specific drawings or photographs. He was gracious enough to spend hours of his time giving personal interviews to the various contributors to this book, and even provided some of his own writing about several of the projects featured. Mr. Krisel also assisted with the book design and image selection which is perfectly consistent with the way he practiced architecture, as he was involved with every aspect of a project's development, including interior design, paint colors, built-in furniture, cupboard handle designs, light switch placement, graphic design for marketing brochures, and site design, including lighting, landscape architecture, stonework, and more. He is generous and exacting, detailed and organized. It is quite remarkable, especially considering that we have had to remind ourselves that Mr. Krisel is ninety-one years old.

As is the nature of collaborative efforts, we would like to acknowledge the following institutions, their staff members, and other individuals who have so patiently assisted us: Sarah Sherman, Ted Walbye, and staff at the Getty Research Institute Research Library; Erin Chase and staff at the Huntington Library; Jonathan Eaker at the Library of Congress; the staff at Gibbs Smith, including publisher Gibbs Smith, contract administrator Michelle Branson, and most especially, patient editor Bob Cooper; and a special thank you to Gary Wexler, book designer, whose creative eye inspired us.

It is also a testament to Mr. Krisel that every writer and photographer whom we approached about contributing to this project plunged in immediately and enthusiastically. We would like to acknowledge the work of the following writers whose expertise broadens an understanding of this architecture and whose separate and distinct voices animated the discourse, whether outright, throughout the chapters of this book, or behind the scenes with their generous advice and support. They are Wim de Wit, Alan Hess, Jim Harlan, Sian Winship, Jim West, Barbara Lamprecht, J. C. Miller, and Jake Gorst, with generous contributions by architectural historians John Crosse and Bethany Morse, architects Alvin Huang, Zoltan Pali, and Steven Ehrlich, and Peter Laszlo, son of the late architect Paul Laszlo.

The architectural photographers whose work is featured in this book include the late Julius Shulman, James Schnepf, and most especially, Darren Bradley. Darren shot more than six hundred photographs of Krisel buildings and worked tirelessly to ensure that both archival and contemporary images were in the very best condition for publication in this book. These creative images, whether historical and artistic records, as in the case of Julius Shulman, or contemporary expressions of what Krisel's work inspires today, are a privilege to feature in our book.

We would also like to acknowledge the generous contributions of images from The Henry Ford; Gamma Rapho, Paris; Hofstra University's Department of Special Collections, Long Island Studies Institute; the Victor Gruen Papers at the American Heritage Center, University of Wyoming; the West-Prinzmetal Architectural Archives, Palm Desert, California; and John Ellis, Patrick Ketchum, Jake and Tracey Gorst, Ron Krisel, Lance Gerber, Marc Treib, Henry Connell, Gary Wexler, Danny Heller, and Peter Siegel and Jon Patrick of Kings Point, Palm Springs, California.

On this project, there are a number of people who have had supportive but important roles. They include our friends and family members. We would like to thank Sigrid and Ellen Creighton, Celia Sylvester, Ellen Cartwright, Frank Winsor, Alan Duncan, Karen Prinzmetal, and Peter Moruzzi, and especially, Mrs. Corinne Krisel, who generously let us intrude into her life and endured our interruptions for months.

Chris and I would like to write a special thank you to Mr. Krisel. It is a privilege to know you and to work with you. We hope to continue the journey, as there is so much more to explore.

Mr. Krisel would like to profusely thank his wife, Corinne (as they begin their sixty-first year of marriage together), for allowing him to be totally "Bill" and to be able to "do it [his] way," yet always being there for support and valued advice.

And finally, Mr. Krisel sends a great thank you to the people of Palm Springs and the other valley cities for their true love of Krisel Modernism and for "keeping the 'language' alive and well."

ingredients for an extraordinary career

SIAN WINSHIP

"I met men from all over the USA and from all walks of life ... all of which I had not previously experienced. From this experience I became even more dedicated to creating well-designed modern homes for the masses."

— WILLIAM KRISEL, ON HIS TIME IN BASIC TRAINING DURING WORLD WAR II

William Krisel (1924–) has calculated that over 40,000 living units of his design have been built.[1] Few architects can make such a monumental statement. Of these buildings, more than 1,500 of them are located in Palm Springs and Palm Desert[2] and largely the result of collaborations with developers of tract homes or condominiums.[3]

The design of postwar merchant-built housing was a task that Krisel was keenly suited for. Born at the nexus of art, technology, replication, and distribution, Krisel was surrounded by all of the elements necessary for success and the innate talent to master it. Every phase of Krisel's spectacular life — his childhood, his military service, his education and early employment history, and his coming of age as an architect during the prosperous postwar period — uniquely prepared him to fulfill America's dream of postwar modern living.

William Krisel was born in Shanghai, China, on November 14, 1924. His father, Alexander Krisel, was a member of the U.S. Consular Service, a federal judge, and a trademark/patent protection attorney who lived in China during the early 1910s. By the time William was born, the elder Krisel was working as the distributor of United Artists motion pictures throughout the region. Ultimately, Al Krisel handled regional distribution for all the major American and French movie studios (which enjoyed a virtual monopoly in the film industry at the time).

Affluent and living in the cosmopolitan French Concession, the Krisels were surrounded by diverse nationalities in the city known as the "Paris of the East." United Artists cofounders Douglas Fairbanks, Mary Pickford, and Charlie Chaplin were all guests of the Krisels in Shanghai. Every two years or so, the Krisel family made trips back to Los Angeles so

Facing: Corinne Krisel (left) with Jill Alexander in the newly completed Alexander Residence, Palm Springs, California, which Corinne furnished (1956)—detail.

Photograph by Julius Shulman. Gift of William and Corinne Krisel. William Krisel Architectural Archive, Getty Research Institute, Los Angeles (2009.M.23). © J. Paul Getty Trust.

RESIDENCE FOR
MR & MRS ALEXANDER KRISEL
RANCHO SANTA FE, CALIFORNIA

VIEW FROM VIA DE FORTUNA

LILIAN J. RICE, ARCHITECT

Front elevation of Alexander Krisel Residence (Lilian J. Rice, unbuilt) in Rancho Santa Fe, California (1934). This was William Krisel's first formal exposure to the architecture profession.

Courtesy of Ron Krisel.

that Al Krisel could negotiate distribution for upcoming films. On these occasions, the Krisel family were the extended houseguests of Pickford and Fairbanks at their legendary Pickfair mansion.

In Shanghai, the Krisel family lived across the street from Madame Chiang Kai-shek. William Krisel remembers, "whenever her limo came out of her gate and if I were on my bike in the street, she would have the driver stop, put down her window and say hello and ask how the family was. She was very, very 'Western' in her daily life. A very charming lady."[4] For the young Krisel, the extraordinary was the ordinary. As a child, he was fluent in English, Mandarin, and the Shanghai and Szechuan Chinese dialects. In July 1937, with the Second Sino-Japanese War on the horizon,

William Krisel and his family left Shanghai on the Japanese luxury liner MS *Asama Maru* and returned permanently to the United States.[5]

Krisel's official introduction to architecture began with his father's purchase of twenty-three acres in Rancho Santa Fe, California, and the engagement of architect Lilian J. Rice (1889–1938) to design a Spanish Colonial Revival ranch. As his father worked with Rice on the design of the ranch, the young Krisel made sketches of his father's changes and they were sent to Rice. As described in the documentary film *William Krisel, Architect,* Krisel recalls, "She made a statement that 'he shows talent . . . he should be an architect.'"[7] Unofficially, Krisel was exposed to the work of Frank Lloyd Wright on the family's trips to and from the United States, during which, according to Krisel, their family routinely stayed at Wright's Imperial Hotel in Tokyo.[8]

In 1938, the thirteen-year-old Krisel took it upon himself to write a letter to the editor of *Time* with suggestions for Franklin D. Roosevelt's home in Hyde Park, the plans for which the magazine had published in weeks prior.

In return, the magazine provided Krisel his first architectural critique: "TIME applauds Student Krisel's attempt but prefers Franklin Roosevelt's own plans of his Hyde Park 'dream house.' Some objections to the Krisel plan: the kitchen is too narrow, the pantry at the wrong end, windows badly spaced, partitions awkwardly arranged; and there is no way into the farther bedroom except through the nearer one.—ED."[9]

Ultimately the Krisels decided not to build the Rancho Santa Fe home. Instead they purchased a home in Beverly Hills across the street from Pickfair, where they added Charlie Chaplin and Fred Astaire to their list of famous neighbors. There, William Krisel established "an architectural studio in the maid's room," where he found discarded renderings for a new house for legendary film director King Vidor (the home's previous renter).[10] While attending Beverly Hills High School, Krisel shaped his own course of architectural study with a mechanical drawing teacher. He graduated at the age of sixteen. With the help of his father, he also managed to net a sunrise to sunset driver's license prior to becoming of legal driving age.[11] Krisel's can-do mentality was supported at an early age, although Al Krisel established high expectations for his son's dedication, hard work, performance, and achievement.[12] All of these values, along with his exposure to his father's business, where art, technology, replication, and distribution coalesced, served the future architect well in his merchant-built housing career.

On the advice of architect Cornelius (Neil) Deasy, who suggested that if Krisel wanted to work in Southern California he should get educated locally, Krisel opted for the USC School of Architecture over Cornell University and began studying there in 1941.[13] After Pearl Harbor, he enlisted in the Army Reserve. When he turned eighteen, his studies were interrupted when he was called up for active duty. After completion of basic training at Camp Santa Anita, Krisel was tapped for his Chinese language skills and sent to the Army Special Training Program at Pomona College, where he was trained as an interpreter for intelligence gathering. Three months later, Private First Class Krisel was sent to serve with General Joseph W. "Vinegar Joe" Stilwell, commander of the China-Burma-India Theater of World War II. In this post, Krisel served as interpreter for the Army's highest-ranking officials and VIPs. He quickly rose to the rank of master sergeant, and when General Stilwell was sent to Okinawa, Krisel remained in China to act as an interpreter for the United States Army Observation Group to

Yan'an, Shanxi Province. For his valorous service to the war effort, Krisel was awarded a Bronze Star by President Harry S. Truman.

Although he was not involved in any military construction, Krisel's military service had a profound effect on him, and ultimately, on his architecture. His time in basic training exposed him to GIs as vastly different as Harvard graduates and men without any formal education. As Krisel described, "I met men from all over the USA and from all walks of life . . . all of which I had not previously experienced. From this experience I became even more dedicated to creating well-designed modern homes for the masses."[14]

Krisel was honorably discharged from military service on Christmas Day 1945. In early 1946, he returned to his studies at USC. In addition to the valuable networking opportunities USC provided, Krisel selected the university for its dedication to Modern architecture.[15] "When I visited the School of Architecture in my senior year [of high school]," Krisel has said, "I saw the projects that the students were doing and was most impressed with the various techniques of presentation but mainly that each project I saw was in the Modern language."[16] He also appreciated the emphasis on design versus engineering. At USC, Krisel's mentors included Maynard Lyndon, Garrett Eckbo, and his prewar fellow-student-turned-instructor, Calvin Straub.[17]

Krisel's perspective drawing teacher, Verle Annis, was another important influence. Annis taught the Shades and Shadows course. In school, Krisel quickly realized that he liked presentations that offered him the opportunity to do perspectives. According to Krisel, Annis's class "opened up a world of three dimensions," and other former students described Annis's contribution as "giving people technically important visualization skills."[18] Krisel augmented his architectural education with elective classes in watercolors, painting, and ceramics. Cultivating his natural talents and honing these skills would serve Krisel well as an architect for merchant builders, wherein the ability to quickly and beautifully execute perspective drawings was an important tool for selling architectural designs to developers, persuading lenders, and ultimately engaging the buying public. Krisel's drawings exuded elegance and a playful optimism that reflected the zeitgeist of the postwar period.

Krisel graduated from USC in 1949 with honors. He was Tau Sigma Delta and was corecipient of the AIA Medal for excellence in design.[19]

Before the war, while Krisel was beginning his studies at USC, he approached the designer Paul Laszlo (1900–93) at his Beverly Hills office and offered himself "as an office boy for no pay."[20] He was immediately hired to do part-time work for twenty hours per week. The Hungarian-born Laszlo had immigrated to the United States in 1936 to escape persecution in Nazi Germany. Although trained at the State Academy of Fine Arts and Design in Stuttgart, Germany, Krisel appreciated that Laszlo "brought Bauhaus ideas" that coincided with Krisel's own interests in Modern architecture.[21]

From Laszlo, Krisel learned about residential architecture and custom homes. Laszlo appreciated the American dream: "I understand the desire of my fellow men to turn their immediate surroundings into a little paradise and I enjoy doing it for them. I love this dream of theirs, and I dream it with them, which is why the home I make will be a joy for them all their life long."[22]

This philosophy would be influential on the young Krisel. "Laszlo was a good architect, but a bad salesman," Krisel recalled. Ultimately, the young apprentice was responsible for creating Laszlo's distinctive "pL" logo that the designer used extensively in marketing his Modern furniture line. While in Laszlo's office, Krisel also prepared drawings for the Desert Comber's Club (Paul Laszlo, 1947). This project would provide inspiration for his work a decade later on Ocotillo Lodge (Palmer & Krisel, 1957).[23]

When Krisel resumed his studies after the war, he continued to work part-time, as a draftsman for the Modern architect Victor Gruen (1903–80). Gruen was an Austrian émigré who fled that country in 1938. In both Laszlo and Gruen, Krisel's choice of mentors reflected his interest in European-rooted avant-garde design. During Krisel's employment from 1946–49, the firm was known as Gruen and Krummeck.[24] At the time, Gruen, who had designed elegant Modern retail stores in Vienna and New York,[25] received the commission for Milliron's department store (Gruen and Krummeck, 1949). During his time with Gruen, Krisel observed both Milliron's design and construction.

Milliron's was revolutionary for a suburban department store. Located in the middle of the burgeoning Westchester postwar suburb, the store sold low- to medium-priced merchandise suited to the tract house–owning population around it. On the busy Sepulveda Boulevard elevation, Gruen conceived four elegant and integrated stage-lit pavilions angled to make their wares more visible to passing motorists and animate the facade.[26] Small glass showcases,

or vitrines, of merchandise were also placed near the auto-motive entrance ramps at the sides of the building. The design deeply impressed Krisel, who remembers: "I had no part in the design of Milliron's but was lucky to be able to even work on it."[27] Gruen's expressive yet elegant street facade for Milliron's linked good architectural design with product sales and the automobile—foreshadowing Krisel's later residential tracts and their engaging architectural cadence from the street.

In contrast to Laszlo, Krisel observed Gruen to be very per-suasive with clients.[28] As architectural historian Richard Longstreth points out in his book *City Center to Regional Mall,* "Gruen's strength was his ability to translate theory into practice—to adapt the radical notions of form and space nurtured by the avant-garde to the pragmatic needs of the merchant and the investor, while making the ideas seem as if they originated with retail concerns.[29]

From his two Modernist mentors, Krisel had gleaned an appreciation for the house as "a little paradise," the Modern

Above, left: Milliron's department store (Gruen and Krummeck, 1949).

Photograph by Julius Shulman.
Getty Research Institute, Los Angeles
(2004.R.10). © J. Paul Getty Trust.

Above, right: Portrait of Victor Gruen (undated).

Victor Gruen Papers, American Heritage Center,
University of Wyoming.

The Falk Apartments, Los Angeles, California, where Palmer & Krisel had their first office.

retail store as an object of auto-friendly merchandising, and how to merge avant-garde design with the needs of investors. These qualities were excellent foundations for building a successful architectural practice with developers. At Gruen and Krummeck, Krisel also met Dan Saxon Palmer (1920–2007), with whom he would form a long-term partnership in 1949.

Dan Saxon Palmer (aka Dan Weissinger) was a Hungarian-born graduate of New York University (1942). Prior to working at Gruen and Krummeck, he worked for three years as a draftsman for Morris Lapidus and Seymour R. Joseph in Florida. At the time of Palmer and Krisel's partnership, Palmer was living in the T. S. Falk Apartments (R. M. Schindler, 1939–40). To save money, the budding young architects excavated an area beneath the Falk Apartments by hand and set up shop—complete with dirt floor. When Krisel's father saw the rustic office conditions, Al Krisel agreed to financially stake the young architects in a proper office by providing the first month's rent.[30] Krisel was not yet licensed as an architect when he and Palmer began the firm.[31] In 1950, he became a licensed architect in the state of California, and in 1954, a licensed landscape architect. In 1955, Krisel obtained an architectural license for all fifty states from the National Council of Architectural Registration Boards.

Of all the prewar Schindler buildings to be working out of, the Falk Apartments may have proved inspirational. Each apartment on the hillside site was oriented to the view and sunlight from the south, and the overall result was a twisting, turning sculptural form from Schindler's Cubist period. Similarly, issues of siting, view corridors, and light as achieved by the placement of volumes in plan would ultimately dominate and differentiate Krisel's residential work.

Palmer and Krisel established a brief and early partnership with John C. Lindsay (1918–78), and their firm was known

William Krisel (left) and Dan Palmer outside their San Vicente Boulevard office, Los Angeles, California (circa 1950).

Collection of William and Corinne Krisel.

Facing: Corinne and William Krisel in their first home, a Corbin Palms tract house in Woodland Hills, California, that Krisel designed (circa 1953).

Collection of William and Corinne Krisel.

as Palmer, Krisel & Lindsay. Important commissions of this period included the Brown Center Medical and Professional Building (Palmer, Krisel & Lindsay, 1951) and the Florence Hawkins Residence (Palmer, Krisel & Lindsay, 1951)—both of which featured butterfly roofs and garnered media coverage in the *Los Angeles Times.* After one year John Lindsay departed the firm, and Palmer & Krisel soon received a series of commissions for tract home developments.

Before long, Krisel's work was featured nationally in prestigious architectural trade publications such as *Arts & Architecture, Architectural Record, Architectural Forum,* and *Progressive Architecture.* During the mid- to late 1950s, Palmer & Krisel also received national Awards of Merit from the National Association of Home Builders for their designs in the San Fernando Valley, Orange County, and Palm Springs for builders such as Harlan Lee, Jerry Snyder and Max Levine, Lawrence Weinberg, and George and Robert Alexander. Even a subdivision house in El Paso, Texas, was honored. All were featured extensively in *House and Home* magazine. During this period, the work of the young architects also steadily appeared in the *Los Angeles Times*—including an article in Esther McCoy's important "What I Believe" series, in which she writes about how the firm "has helped give distinction to the tract house."[32] Palmer & Krisel was one of the few firms in the nation that managed to bridge the worlds of architectural high design, merchant builders, and homebuyers.

In 1953, William Krisel married Corinne R. Jaffe (1933–). In addition to keeping the home fires burning and raising their two children, Corinne often contributed to the firm's unique value proposition as "one coordinated effort" for its developer clients. Palmer & Krisel provided complete interior supervision, graphic design, display materials, and sales brochures. Although Palmer & Krisel often teamed up with noted color consultant and designer C. Tony Pereira,

William Krisel and Abraham Shapiro (fourth and fifth from left), Krisel/Shapiro & Associates (circa 1969).

Collection of William and Corinne Krisel.

Corinne also periodically provided color or interior design services for the firm.

By 1964, Palmer and Krisel were effectively operating independently, with separate offices and separate clients. That same year, Krisel opened independent offices in San Diego and West Los Angeles. According to Krisel, however, his partnership with Dan Saxon Palmer wasn't officially dissolved until 1966. Krisel established a solo practice for three years and during this period designed many projects in the Coachella Valley. In 1969 he formed a new partnership with Abraham Shapiro (1925–). Shapiro was born in Tel Aviv and educated at the Hebrew Institute of Technology. He also earned a master's degree in architecture from Columbia in 1953. At the time of the partnership, Shapiro had significant experience in commercial high-rise design and construction which Krisel did not. By the late 1960s, developers were increasingly looking to high-rise residential buildings as an answer to the needs of "empty nesters," who now craved recreational amenities, more urban locations, and fewer maintenance responsibilities. The partnership yielded a number of significant residential high-rise works, including the Ocean Avenue Towers (Krisel/Shapiro & Associates, 1971) in Santa Monica and

Coronado Shores (Krisel/Shapiro & Associates, 1972–78) in the San Diego area.

In 1979, the increasingly litigious nature of architectural practice compelled Krisel to sell his share of the practice to Shapiro. From 1980 onward, Krisel acted as a consultant for housing and forensic architecture, first with A. C. Martin and Associates and later as an independent consultant.

Krisel's childhood prepared him well for respecting other cultures and mediating between them. In adulthood, his wartime experience put him in touch with the common man in ways he had not previously known. Ultimately, Krisel's artistic talent, relentless drive, and keen business mind compelled him to become an effective translator between uncompromising architectural design and the developer community—a unique genius among a generation of postwar architects. The timelessness of Krisel's designs has also revealed itself to a new generation of enthusiasts and owners who have embraced his work, designated his buildings as historic resources, and bestowed new awards on him. His Palm Springs legacy is but one chapter in a spectacular life and a robust career as one of Southern California's most significant Modern architects.

NOTES

1. Robert Imber and David Shearer, *Visions of Utopia* (Palm Springs, CA: Palm Springs Desert Museum, 2004), 13.

2. According to the architect himself, his Coachella Valley projects represented only approximately 7 percent of the total dollar volume of his career.

3. Calculations by the author as informed by James R. Harlan's book *The Alexanders: A Desert Legacy* (Palm Springs, CA: Palm Springs Preservation Foundation, 2011).

4. John Crosse, "William Krisel and George Alexander in Hollywood, 1937–1956," *Southern California Architectural History* (blog), January 13, 2011, socalarchhistory.blogspot.com/2011/01/william-krisel-and-george-alexanders.html.

5. *Selected Passenger and Crew Lists and Manifests, M1764—Los Angeles, Selected Suburbs, 1907–1948,* Image 79. National Archives, Washington, D.C.

6. "Letters," *Time,* November 14, 1938. www.time.com/time/magazine/article/0,9171,771997,00.html.

7. *William Krisel, Architect,* DVD (2 disks), produced by Jill A. Wiltse, H. Kirk Brown III, and Heather Purcell; directed by Jake Gorst (Denver, CO: Design Onscreen, 2010).

8. William Krisel, interview with Sian Winship, February 2, 2011.

9. "Letters," *Time,* November 14, 1938.

10. Crosse, "William Krisel and George Alexander in Hollywood, 1937–1956."

11. Ibid.

12. In the film *William Krisel, Architect,* he describes his father's disappointed reaction to a report card with four A grades and one B grade as "What happened?" and his father's follow-up reaction to a report card with all A grades as "Now you have to keep it up."

13. Krisel, interview.

14. William Krisel, e-mail to Sian Winship, February 26, 2011.

15. At this time, most schools of architecture were still using the traditional Beaux Arts curriculum.

16. Deborah Howell-Ardila, "'Writing our own program': the USC experiment in modern architectural pedagogy, 1930 to 1960" (MHP thesis, University of Southern California, 2010), 108.

17. William Krisel, e-mail to Sian Winship, May 5, 2011.

18. Howell-Ardila, "Writing Our Own Program," 178.

19. "Architects Win Awards," *Daily Trojan,* May 18, 1949, 3.

20. Krisel, interview.

21. Ibid.

22. Sian Winship, *Exiles and Emigres in Los Angeles Modernist Architecture* (Sherman Oaks, CA: Society of Architectural Historians/Southern California Chapter, 1997), 4.

23. Crosse, "William Krisel and George Alexander in Hollywood, 1937–1956."

24. Victor Gruen was married to Elsie Krummeck.

25. Alex Wall, *Victor Gruen: From Urban Shop to New City* (Barcelona, Spain: ActarD, 2005), 30.

26. M. Jeffrey Hardwick, *Mall Maker: Victor Gruen, Architect of an American Dream* (Philadelphia: University of Pennsylvania Press, 2004), 72–117.

27. Krisel, interview.

28. Ibid.

29. Richard Longstreth, *City Center to Regional Mall:* Architecture, the Automobile, and Retailing in Los Angeles, 1920–1950 (Cambridge, MA: MIT Press, 1998), 323.

30. Crosse, "William Krisel and George Alexander in Hollywood, 1937–1956."

31. John Crosse, *William Krisel Oral History* (Playa del Rey, CA: modern-ISM Press, 2009), 92.

32. Esther McCoy, "What I Believe: A Statement of Palmer and Krisel's Architectural Principles," *Los Angeles Times,* May 20, 1956, 4.

modernism is a language

ALAN HESS

The Dymaxion House
at its 1948–91 site,
near Andover, Kansas.

"Taliesin was not real life" — **WILLIAM KRISEL, INTERVIEW WITH ALAN HESS (JULY 15, 2015)**

Midcentury Modernists in California didn't write about their architectural theories. They built them.

William Krisel is a key example. Throughout his education and practice he continually explored, refined, and redefined Modernist concepts. In his mass-produced housing tracts he mastered both the construction technology and rational management systems of the Industrial Revolution, adapting them creatively to new conditions. He helped to perfect the modern tract home, the basic building block of the modern suburban metropolises growing after 1945. He did so by building homes with Modernist open plans, filled with light, suited to Modernist lifestyles, and he built them for the masses by skillfully applying Modernist concepts like modularization and prefabrication. He worked at the interface of the pragmatic economics of the demanding home building industry and sophisticated Modernist design. To Krisel, Modernism was a problem-solving process more than an aesthetic. He pushed that process as far as any California architect in the midcentury period—an era known for an abundance of talented and inventive architects.

Histories tend to favor architects who write concise theoretical manifestos, however. The scarcity of such manifestos from midcentury California has hampered our full appreciation of the innovations of its architecture. But today, in looking at the careers of Krisel and many of his colleagues, we can see how they pushed their ideas past what was typical (or even acceptable) for the profession at the time. They were Modernist pioneers, inventors, and mavericks.

Facing: View of the Signature House designed by Krisel for the 1956 Los Angeles Home Show (1956). It featured many of the design elements that would appear in Krisel's Palm Springs projects.

Photograph by Julius Shulman.
Getty Research Institute, Los Angeles
(2004.R.10). © J. Paul Getty Trust.

Krisel's own restless intellect was well suited to the challenges of Modernism. In 1950, he and his new partner Dan Saxon Palmer decided to focus on the mass-produced tract housing industry, a field that most architects (including the poo-bahs of the American Institute of Architects) considered beneath the dignity of serious architects.

The application of Modernist design theory to mass-produced housing remained largely unrealized in practice. There were many theoretical (and utopian) proposals: Buckminster Fuller's Dymaxion House, for example, ingeniously addressed how to build mass-produced houses in a factory. Two other noted architects, Walter Gropius and Konrad Wachsmann, addressed the issue of prefabrication with their General Panel System, which Krisel learned in architecture school at USC (where Wachsmann later taught). In school, Krisel was impressed. "This is going to solve all this problem [of prefabrication]," he thought.[1] When he later learned the real problems of the housing industry, however, he changed his mind.

Between the narrow pragmatism of builders ("You're wasting your time," they told Krisel) and the architecture profession's biases, Krisel mapped out a third way. Fuller, Gropius, and Wachsmann solved just one technical problem: how to fabricate buildings in mass quantities. Krisel went further by applying Modernist principles to the commercial realities of the entire building process.

His intent was clear: to create Modern living spaces using Modern methods and materials. He and Palmer learned and analyzed each step in the process to determine how Modernist design could cut costs and deliver value using new forms and methods. By listening closely to his builder clients, he addressed their need for speedy, uncomplicated construction, and ways to cut costs—all through using Modernist methods. "We deferred to the Alexanders [clients

George and Robert Alexander] as to what the program would be," he explains.

This was the kind of intricate juggling act that attracted Krisel. It was the essence of Modernist problem-solving as he defined it. And when Palmer and Krisel's first Modern tract made more money for the Alexander Construction Company than a traditional tract, they were on their way to winning over the hard-nosed builder clients.

As all good Modernists knew, form follows function. Krisel applied that concept more broadly than most architects.

Krisel's designs included plans as cutting edge as any in Southern California: open plans united kitchen, dining room, living room, and outdoor patios to serve the informal lifestyles emerging after World War II. Instead of traditional boxy rooms, he designed sloping ceilings and clerestory windows that spread natural air and light through his houses.

He then went beyond the customary functions of a house by also addressing the economic functions in the building process that shaped designs and constrained methods of construction. The building industry was already using the basics of modern assembly-line production: repetitive elements, prefabrication, and the rationalized management of time, materials, and labor. Krisel determined to use those industrial elements—growing out of the Industrial Revolution itself—to create true Modernist architecture that was more than an aesthetic of clean lines and machine imagery. It was a rational, scientific methodology that employed empirical observation to improve on conventional practices.

For example, he used prefabrication, but only by carefully selecting discrete elements to be prefabricated (doors, windows, and kitchen and bathroom modules, for example) where costs could be reduced and construction accelerated.

These elements were set in a modularized plan where material use could be optimized, reducing waste. The post-and-beam construction system Krisel learned under Calvin Straub at USC also maximized materials by concentrating the structure in a framework, leaving the other walls non-load bearing, and speeding construction.

Beyond construction methods, Krisel also learned the housing industry's other real-world functions and integrated them into a new equation. These included land acquisition, marketing, cost analysis, financing, landscaping, advertising, brochures, graphics, interiors, marketable amenities, and the design of sales offices. Palmer & Krisel offered clients the tract housing industry equivalent of "Total Design," the concept that Welton Becket and Associates, a much larger commercial firm, developed to serve their corporate and institutional clients.

A few other respected Modernist architects around 1950 also designed tracts, though Palmer & Krisel's work stands

Street view, Alexander-built houses (Palmer & Krisel) in Twin Palms Estates, Palm Springs, California (circa 1957)—detail.

Photograph by Julius Shulman. Getty Research Institute, Los Angeles (2004.R.10). © J. Paul Getty Trust.

out in volume and sophistication. Like Palmer & Krisel, Cliff May and Chris Choate developed a small-house design that used prefabrication and modular elements; instead of working with builders, however, they sold kits of their houses to developers who would then construct them. Edward H. Fickett worked equally hard to convince builders to use Modernist architecture, though he did not develop the use of prefabrication and modularization that streamlined Palmer & Krisel's work. Anshen & Allen, Jones and Emmons, and Claude Oakland all designed Modernist models for progressive Bay Area developer Joseph Eichler and other large builders. Smith and Williams's wide-ranging practice included Modernist housing tracts also developing open plans and contemporary exteriors.

But the general attitude in the profession was that, while custom home design was a worthy task for architects, mass-produced housing was a tough and commercial industry driven by the bottom line. Designing tract homes was considered a trade, not a gentleman's profession. That's the way it had been practiced, for the most part: commercial builders dictated basic designs to drafting services, which drew up the construction documents exactly as the builder asked. Hiring Modern architects invited complications that would cost time and money, whereas "there were no arguments with a drafting service," Krisel recalls. As a result, few Modern architects saw how to use their innovative structures or create dynamic spaces in a tract home.

Jones and Emmons, as well as Smith and Williams, already had established professional reputations based on a wide variety of building types, so their limited involvement with tract homes did not raise concerns in the profession. Palmer & Krisel, however, was still a young firm without such a track record. Their success in the tract-housing industry brought threats of expulsion from the AIA.

Yet applying modern technology to mass-produced housing was one of Modernism's goals. Embedded in it was another fundamental purpose of Modernism: to use technology to improve the lives of average citizens. "Otherwise who needs it?" Krisel asks. "It has to function and serve the public."

This goal had been on his mind for a while. Chatting with fellow GIs during World War II, he learned that most had transited through Southern California on their way to the Pacific Theater, and they wanted to return there to settle after the war; the weather was so much better than back in Iowa, New Hampshire, or Kentucky. They would need homes that allowed them to enjoy a new way of life.

It might seem surprising that William Krisel, raised in such exotic circumstances (born in the privileged French Concession in Shanghai; later a neighbor of Charlie Chaplin and Fred Astaire in Beverly Hills), should become a practitioner of tract housing for the masses. But while elitism caused many AIA members to turn up their noses at tract housing, Krisel's innate curiosity saw it as an intriguingly complex puzzle that demanded an elegant solution, like the geometry problems in school that he saw as "fun and games." In comparison, he found the design of custom homes boring; counting the number of ties a wealthy client owned was just not satisfying.

Krisel had always been a close observer of his environment. "Everything I did and saw had an influence on me," he says, and he would file it away in his memory for later use. This habit of drawing on actual experience started early, before he even knew what Modernism was. In Shanghai, his family lived in a formal Colonial-style house designed by a French architect (three floors plus a full basement, with fireplaces in every room), but the family would vacation in Japan, at a beach house or a mountain house. Even as a child, the simple practicality and efficient use of space in the

Japanese houses impressed him (as they did many other California architects, including Charles and Henry Greene, and Richard Neutra). Instead of small walk-in closets, the Japanese rooms had an entire wall of wardrobes behind sliding shoji screens. Large drawers for bedding pulled out underneath the shojis. At the beach house, the outer walls were also shoji screens, pulling back to open the indoors to the outdoors. The houses directly expressed their wood frames, held together not with screws or nails, but with wood pegs, joints, and bamboo strapping. Here was the basic Modernist concept of structural expression. "It had a profound effect," Krisel remembers.

In building mass-produced homes, Krisel was also addressing the larger issue of Modernist planning. Housing tracts were one of the basic building blocks of suburbia, the urban form that defined post–World War II America. He was not simply designing individual houses; he was designing an entire neighborhood, its streets and setbacks, its overall appearance. Homebuyers were tiring of the cookie-cutter similarity of early mass-produced housing tracts at Lakewood

and Panorama City, in Southern California, and Levittown, New York. Those tracts disappointed Krisel, too. "They insulted me as an architect," he recalls.

After Palmer & Krisel's initial years learning the tract housing industry and developing strategies, in 1957 the Alexander Construction Company presented the opportunity to put all they had learned together at Twin Palms Estates, a vacation home tract in Palm Springs. "It was the end result of everything I wanted to do," says Krisel. Buyers of second homes were more open to new ideas than those buying in the bedroom communities of the San Fernando Valley, Orange County, and San Diego. By capturing the lifestyle of Palm Springs, they could fully integrate their practical knowledge with the ideals of Modernist design.

In planning Twin Palms, Krisel balanced the advantages of mass production with the appeal of diversity. Each house repeated the identical square plan, taking advantage of the cost savings in repetitive production—but he rotated the

Left: Aerial view of Levittown, New York (circa 1950s).

Reproduced from Hofstra University Special Collections.

Above: View of Baldwin Hills Village, Los Angeles, California, designed by architect Robert Evans Alexander (1958).

Photograph by Julius Shulman. Getty Research Institute, Los Angeles (2004.R.10). © J. Paul Getty Trust.

plan on each site to present a different facade. By offering several roof variations, he created a varied neighborhood that appealed to homebuyers.

A few years later Krisel would expand this Modernist master planning concept at the Sandpiper condominiums in Palm Desert. He was acquainted with master planning theory from working for Gruen and Krummeck (perhaps the most progressive and successful planning and architecture office in the country) in the late 1940s, but he had encountered it earlier at Baldwin Hills Village, a garden apartment project built before the war in Los Angeles. Always a keen observer of the urban environment, Krisel had noticed it under construction on the route he drove from the family's Beverly Hills home to the USC School of Architecture. Instead of the typical tract development divided up into streets and individual lots, it was an entire block with no interior streets, no lot lines, and no fences, planned by architects Reginald Johnson, Lewis Wilson, Edwin Merrill, and Robert Evans Alexander, with landscape architect Fred Barlow Jr. and consultant Clarence Stein. On this broad site the unified plan rearranged the elements of a neighborhood into a new configuration: one- and two-story apartment units around the perimeter, leaving a broad landscaped open space at the center for recreation and beauty; garages were clustered in perimeter courts, and pathways led to houses.

Twenty years later, Krisel would update the concept at Sandpiper by clustering the one-story triplex units around landscaped gardens and swimming pools. It was still a radical idea; he had to convince the planning commission to accept the planned unit development concept, just as he had to convince housing builders to adopt his Modernist tract home design concepts. But he was still committed to Modernism as a set of fundamental theories that went far deeper than their clean, efficient surface appearance.

This synthesis of real-world conditions and Modernist ideals in order to build for the mass public is basic to Krisel's theory of architecture. It is also central to the character of Southern California Modernism. The region's architects were inspired by building in a natural paradise, fearlessly pragmatic in adopting new technology, exploring the experience of modern life, skillful in using the commercial environment of the society. William Krisel's career epitomizes this approach to Modernist design. Though he greatly admired Frank Lloyd Wright (early family vacations took him to the Imperial Hotel in Tokyo, and as a teenager he devoured an *Architectural Forum* issue devoted to Wright), Krisel had decided not to study at Taliesin after an interview with Wright. "Taliesin was not real life," he concluded. The challenge of solving real-world problems remained the source of Krisel's energy and inspiration.

NOTES

1. This and all other direct quotes in this chapter from William Krisel, interview with Alan Hess, July 11, 2015.

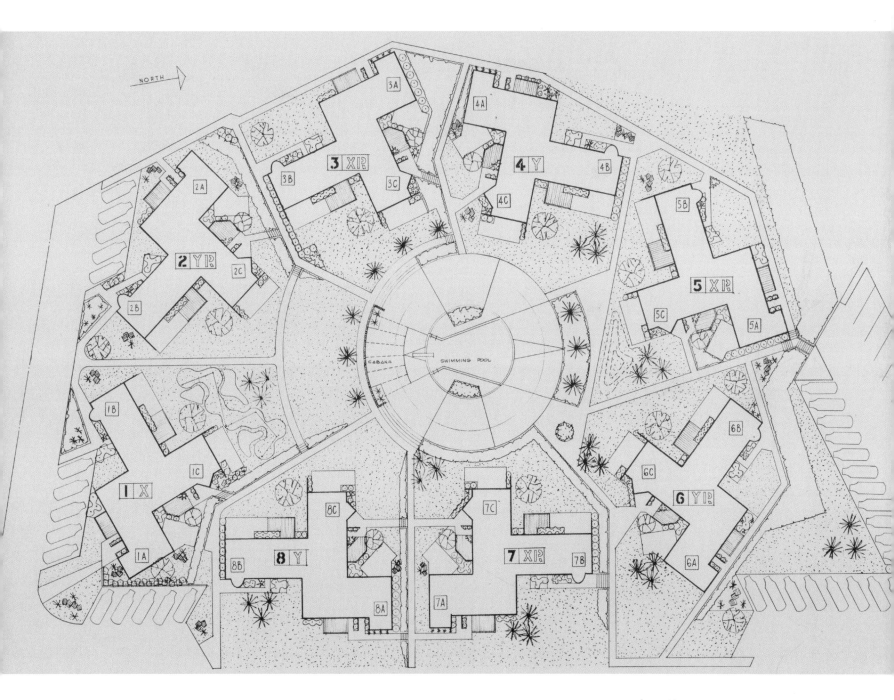

NORTH

3A

4A

3 X

4 Y

4B

3B

3C

4C

2A

5B

2 Y

2C

5 X

5C

5A

2B

SWIMMING POOL

CABANA

1B

6B

6C

1C

6 Y

1 X

6A

8C

7C

1A

7 X

8 Y

7B

8B

8A

7A

6A

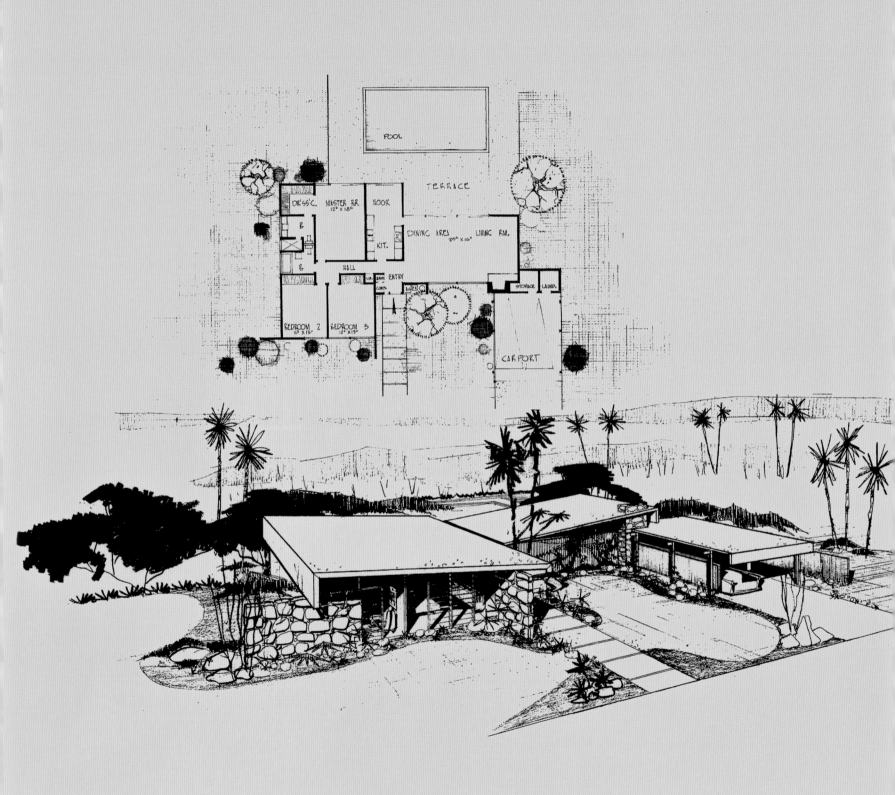

POOL

TERRACE

DR'SS'G. MASTER BR. NOOK
12° X 18°

DINING AREA LIVING RM.
25° X 16°

KIT.

B

B

HALL

ENTRY

STORAGE LAUND.

BEDROOM 2 BEDROOM 3
12° X 15° 12° X 15°

CARPORT

3 on tract

JIM HARLAN

"[It's] significant [that] almost every big name in Modern architecture at midcentury tried to crack into the mass-produced housing market. And they all failed." — **ALAN HESS**

Left: Krisel Residence, Corbin Palms tract, Woodland Hills, California (1953).

Photograph by Julius Shulman. Gift of William and Corinne Krisel. William Krisel Architectural Archive, Getty Research Institute, Los Angeles (2009.M.23). © J. Paul Getty Trust.

Levittown, New York, one of the early postwar tract neighborhoods, was described by architectural historian Lewis Mumford in 1961 as "a multitude of uniform, unidentifiable houses, lined up inflexibly, at uniform distances on uniform roads, in a treeless command waste, inhabited by people of the same class, the same incomes, the same age group, witnessing the same television performance, eating the same tasteless prefabricated foods, from the same freezers, conforming in every outward and inward respect to a common mold manufactured in the same central metropolis.

Thus the ultimate effect of the suburban escape in our time is, ironically, a low-grade uniform environment from which escape is impossible."[1] In fact, social critics and architectural historians for the most part ignored the development of tract housing. "To them these houses did not seem to be 'architecture.'"[2]

With that condemnation, the use of the word "tract" to describe and then market a home, let alone a vacation home in the desert, could hardly have been seen as a wise

Facing: Rendering of tract house with floor plan, Valley of the Sun, Rancho Mirage, California (1957).

Gift of William and Corinne Krisel. William Krisel Architectural Archive, Getty Research Institute, Los Angeles (2009.M.23). © J. Paul Getty Trust.

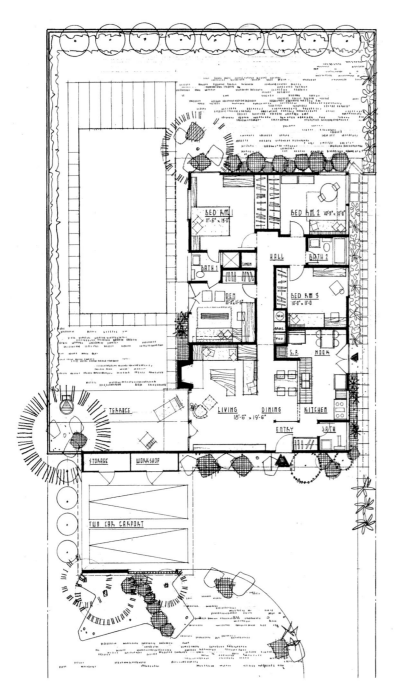

move. However, the Alexander Construction Company, headed by George Alexander and his son Bob, were not new to tract homes, and they certainly understood marketing. But most importantly, they hired William Krisel to design their first tract in the desert.

The Alexanders had worked with Krisel earlier to design several very successful tract home projects in Southern California's San Fernando Valley. The first project, called Corbin Palms, consisted of simple and elegant post-and-beam homes that sold rapidly. With Corbin Palms, Krisel showed the Alexanders how to bring excellent and modern design to mass-produced housing while saving on construction costs, thereby increasing the profitability of the project. "That's significant because almost every big name in Modern architecture at midcentury tried to crack into the mass-produced housing market. And they all failed."[3]

Palm Springs in the 1950s would provide the ingredients necessary to create housing for the growing leisure lifestyle—year-round sunshine, easy access by automobile from Los Angeles and San Diego, inexpensive land, and later, the important introduction of air-conditioning.

Bob and Helene Alexander
(circa 1962).

West-Prinzmetal Architectural
Archives, Palm Desert, California.

George and Bob wisely brought in many of the major sub-contractors that they had worked with in Los Angeles, making them partners in the company. Arguably, that may be the reason for the high level of quality achieved in the developments.

George remained behind the scenes but gave input with regard to major decisions, such as when and where to build. Project locations were chosen wisely and were usually located adjacent to landmarks or well-established neighborhoods. For example, Racquet Club Road Estates was adjacent to the famous Racquet Club resort, and Vista Las Palmas abutted the affluent Las Palmas neighborhood.

Bob Alexander, along with architect Krisel, had carte blanche with regard to the general design and aesthetics of the final, constructed product. This division of labor helped ensure the success of the Alexander Construction Company by clearly defining duties and responsibilities. While the Alexanders have been enthusiastically credited with building as many as 2,500 homes in the Palm Springs area, the actual number is 1,260.

In 1955, George Alexander, in semiretirement, moved to Palm Springs to rest and attend to his health. However, he quickly became restless and, seeing that the growing desert city needed housing, formed the Alexander Construction Company. The new venture was motivated by two factors. First, the construction business in the Los Angeles area had turned highly competitive and opportunities were dwindling. Second, it was apparent that the village of Palm Springs had not yet seen builders as competent and savvy as George and his son and partner Bob.

Bob headed the day-to-day operations of the company and was largely in charge of the Palm Springs operation. Smart and personable, he was the face of the company, appearing in advertisements for the various neighborhood developments. Bob's projects include Twin Palms, Vista Las Palmas, and Racquet Club Road Estates, all designed by William Krisel, the partner in charge of all projects in the Palm Springs area for the architectural firm Palmer & Krisel.

In addition to William Krisel, the Alexanders engaged a host of talented Modernist architects. This set them apart from many other Coachella Valley builders. These well-educated and forward-thinking architects brought a Modernist aesthetic to their homebuilding, and creativity was not bound by either building codes or conventional thinking. For instance, in the Twin Palms tract, permit records show that the firm of Palmer & Krisel sought variances to the building code. One variance allowed an exterior wall to extend beyond the perimeter of the house and into the side-yard setback, creating in essence integral garden walls. Surprisingly, this was done for design purposes only, a rarity for speculative construction of this scale.

Rendering showing examples of
roolines for Racquet Club Road
Estates, Palm Springs, California
(1959)—detail.

Aerial view of the nearly completed homes
in Twin Palms, Palm Springs, California
(circa 1956). Note the variety of rooflines.

Menrad Collection.

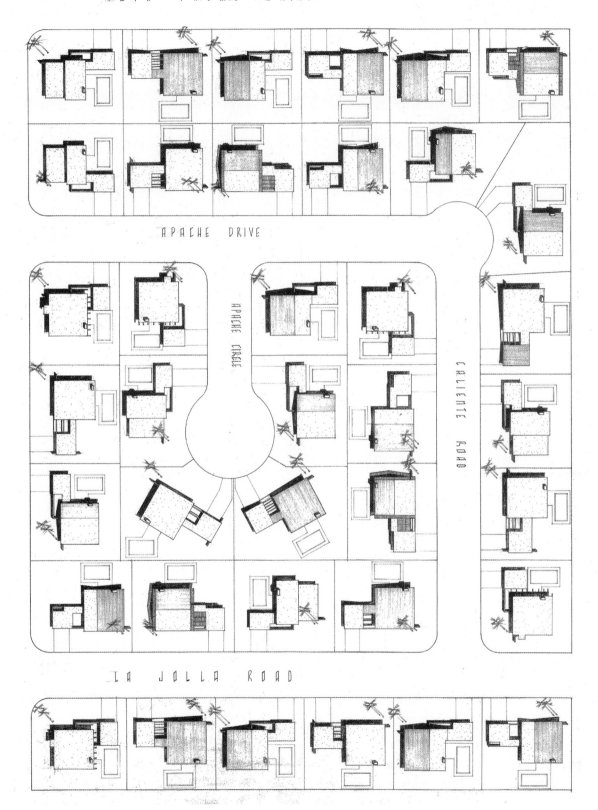

TWIN PALMS DRIVE

APACHE DRIVE

APACHE CIRCLE

CALIENTE ROAD

LA JOLLA ROAD

Plot plan for Twin Palms (1956)—detail. Krisel indicated placement of the two palm trees and swimming pool, but also the precise location of each house on the lot. This assured that the neighborhood had a custom look.

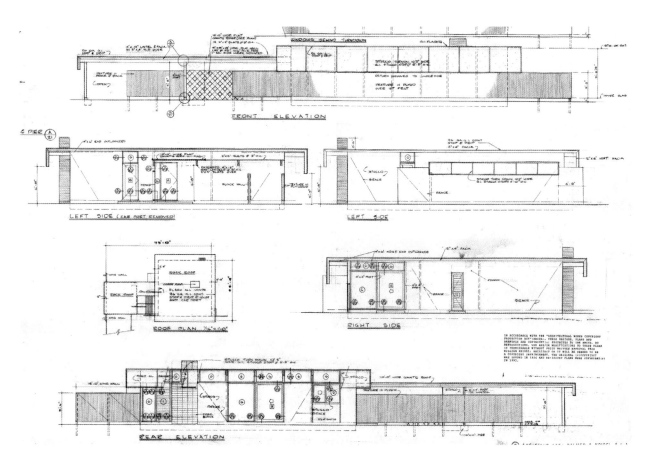

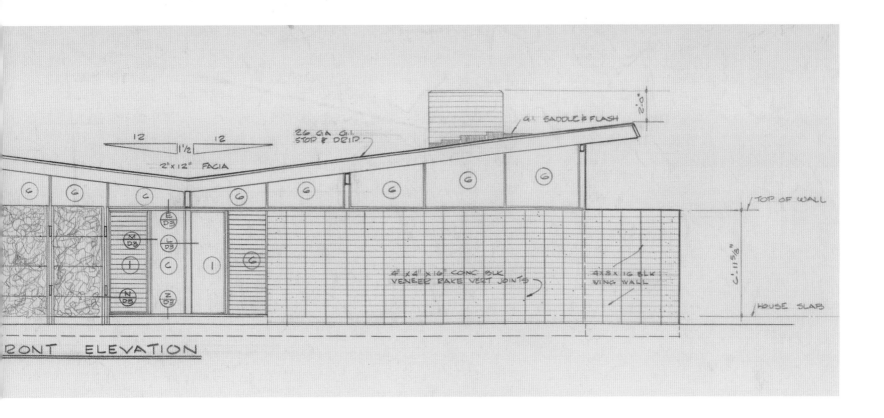

FRONT ELEVATION

Above: Elevation drawing for butterfly roof (Model A-4), Twin Palms, Palm Springs, California (1956)—detail. Note the unique use of Conwood panels providing texture and visual interest at low cost.

Facing: Elevation drawing for sun flap roof (Model A-3), Twin Palms, Palm Springs, California (1956)—detail. Note the T111 plywood siding along the front exterior. This feature extends as wing walls stretching the length of the house on either side.

Gifts of William and Corinne Krisel. William Krisel Architectural Archive, Getty Research Institute, Los Angeles (2009.M.23). © J. Paul Getty Trust.

Right: Exterior view of butterfly-roof tract home, Twin Palms, Palm Springs, California (2012). This home was originally designed in 1956 for Joe Dunas, a partner with the Alexanders in the Twin Palms development.

Photograph © Darren Bradley.

The neighborhood now known as Twin Palms (which includes what used to be known as Smoke Tree Valley Estates, El Camino Estates, and Royal Desert Estates) was the first subdivision designed by William Krisel in Palm Springs. Here, some of the ideas explored earlier at Corbin Palms were taken to the next level. Constructed between 1956 and 1957, the ninety-home tract was completed in three phases. The Alexanders were so delighted with Krisel's new home recently completed in Brentwood, California, that they requested that the new Palm Springs homes incorporate some of the details highlighted there. Such features included atriums, sun flaps and trellis structures to control light, and especially the post-and-beam construction.

Sited on generous 10,000-square-foot lots and constructed on 40 by 40 foot concrete pads, the 1,600-square-foot homes were relatively spacious for their time and featured three bedrooms and two bathrooms. Services were located in the center of the home, creating a linear core punctuated by an atrium off the master bath. This intimate feature invited desert cacti and natural rock forms directly into the home. Nothing like these Twin Palms homes had ever been seen before in the desert. The rooflines (flat, gabled, and inverted) were distinctive and dramatic, and seemed to mimic the shapes of the magnificent mountains in the background. These well-built homes were priced at around $30,000. Each came with a swimming pool and two palm trees in the front yard—thus the name. Twin Palms sold like wildfire!

The Alexanders built their tract homes during the summer months from May to October, when temperatures soared well over 100 degrees. The work crews would begin at 5 a.m. and end at 1 p.m. with a jump in the swimming pool and beer on ice provided by the Alexanders. This scheduling was deliberate, as the houses had to be ready for sale and occupancy when the desert winter season

Racquet Club Road Estates butterfly roofline,
Palm Springs, California (1959).

Rendering of Model A-1, Racquet Club Road Estates,
Palm Springs, California (1958)—detail.

Above: Kitchen arrangement at Racquet Club Road Estates, Palm Springs, California (1959).

Facing: Interior of Racquet Club Road Estates home, Palm Springs, California (1958), showing an open kitchen with movable floating island so that the homeowner could customize the kitchen size.

began, thus avoiding costly interest payments on completed homes and maintenance during the searing summer months.

All of the Krisel-designed homes for the Alexanders were framed in wood. The lumber supplier framed one of each model (there were three different models for Twin Palms), and then made a list of each piece of lumber necessary to completely rough frame the house. The result was a package of all of the lumber required to frame a particular model. The supplier delivered to each lot as soon as the concrete slab floors were poured so that the framing crews could begin work immediately.

Even though there was only one basic floor plan, there were eight different variations to the exteriors, created by employing a variety of rooflines such as the now famous butterfly. In addition, Krisel would rotate the house on the lot, orienting the front door to either an entry courtyard on the side or to the street at the front. Krisel's creative geometry ensured that no two houses were the same. He plotted each house, selected the exterior color scheme, located the two palm trees, designed fences, positioned the swimming pools, and integrated the whole neighborhood so that the homes appeared to the casual observer to be custom designs. His involvement in every aspect of the design and construction process ensured that these tract houses did not have the cookie-cutter look and feel that Mumford and other social critics disapproved of, and also saved the builder money.

Many of the neighborhood tracts that comprise the area now known as Vista Las Palmas were also designed by William Krisel. Started in 1957, it was on the heels of, and even overlapped, much of the construction occurring in Twin Palms. A tract map (identifying Abrigo Road, Via Las Palmas, Vista Vespero, Via Vadera, and Via Monte Vista) for the initial proposed construction in Vista Las Palmas is dated December 21, 1956.

Krisel designed what was to become the largest tract in Palm Springs, the 360-home Racquet Club Road Estates, which derived its name from its proximity to the Racquet Club resort. The resort was founded by Hollywood stars Charlie Farrell and Ralph Bellamy, and had been a Palm Springs social hub since the 1930s. These homes were almost identical to those of Twin Palms in their schematic floor plan except that the scale was somewhat smaller—35 by 35 feet (1,225 square feet). Because of the smaller footprint, the design was cleverly adapted to feature an open kitchen that created the illusion of spaciousness. The Racquet Club Road Estates effort spanned multiple years; dates on the seven plot plans range from August 14, 1958 through October 13, 1960. Krisel specified the location and orientation of each home on these plot plans to create a varied and nonrepetitive tract of beautiful Modernist homes, as he had done in Twin Palms.

In 1957, Krisel worked with a different builder on a project of twelve homes named Valley of the Sun located in nearby Rancho Mirage. Developers Maus & Holstein (the land was owned by Maus) built the homes on two cul-de-sacs, each with six lots. Later, two more homes were added, as Holstein's superintendent at the Sandpiper, who was also in charge of the construction at Rancho Mirage, wanted Krisel homes of his own.

Two floor plans were implemented for the twelve-unit development, both 1,600 square feet. Each floor plan had four different and distinct elevations. Again, as in previous projects, exterior materials ranged greatly from model to model. Carports were pulled forward and back, all to create a varied look.

The city of Palm Springs has experienced a rebirth in part because of a burgeoning appreciation for the tracts of superbly designed Modernist homes by William Krisel.

Backyard view of Racquet Club Road Estates house,
Palm Springs, California (1959)—detail.

Mostly built by the Alexander Construction Company, these midcentury housing developments of modest single-family homes are now properly viewed as an integral element of the midcentury architecture for which the city is now internationally known.

So it is that nearly sixty years after they were built, the interest in Krisel homes is very strong. Many of the homes have been renovated to match their original designs, garnering numerous awards in the process. The cultural heritage boards of Palm Springs, Rancho Mirage, and Palm Desert have stepped up efforts to protect the homes by designating many of them as historical landmarks. The enjoyment derived from living in these homes today, aided by the ease with which new technologies can be incorporated into the original designs, is a tribute to the architect and his language of Modernism.

NOTES

1. Lewis Mumford, *The City in History: Its Origins, Its Transformations, and Its Prospects* (New York: Harcourt, Brace & World, 1961), 486.

2. Barbara Miller Lane, *Houses for a New World: Builders and Buyers in American Suburbs, 1945–1965* (Princeton, NJ: Princeton University Press, 2015), 29.

3. Alan Hess, in discussion with Heidi Creighton, February 20, 2015.

Tract house with flat roof built in 1956

in Twin Palms, Palm Springs, California

(2012).

Photograph © Darren Bradley.

View of a Model B-4 home (circa 1957), Valley of the Sun,
Rancho Mirage, California (2012). The nonoriginal screen
block was added at a later date.

Photograph © Darren Bradley.

Rendering of Valley of the Sun house, Rancho
Mirage, California (circa 1957)—detail.

Presentation rendering of a poolside view
at Ocotillo Lodge (circa 1956)—detail.

ocotillo lodge

CHRIS MENRAD

"Architecture is not just an intellectual exercise—it is an emotional exercise also. That beyond the versatility and professionalism of the architect, there must also be a bright and poetic mind involved with each project."

— **WILLIAM KRISEL, E-MAIL TO HEIDI CREIGHTON (2015)**

Early concept rendering of Ocotillo Lodge's diamond-shaped porte cochere (circa 1957).

Gift of William and Corinne Krisel.
William Krisel Architectural Archive,
Getty Research Institute,
Los Angeles (2009.M.23).
© J. Paul Getty Trust.

In 1954, George and Bob Alexander purchased land in Palm Springs located just two miles south of downtown. The Alexanders saw Palm Springs as a new market where they could offer the middle class, for the first time, a holiday destination with the same lifestyle attractions that the well-to-do were already enjoying. Their company had already built single-family tract homes, apartments, and offices in Los Angeles. They could do the same thing here, only with virtually no competition. At the time, it was a wide-open market for them, and their new Palm Springs venture would soon change the face of the town.

Ocotillo Lodge was conceived by the father and son team not only as a new investment in Palm Springs but also as a

Bob and Helene Alexander's
residence in Twin Palms,
Palm Springs, California,
featured a long butterfly roof
(1957)—detail.

Photograph by Julius Shulman.
Getty Research Institute,
Los Angeles (2004.R.10).
© J. Paul Getty Trust.

way to market the new homes that they were building. The new neighborhood was then called Smoke Tree Valley Estates (it's now part of what's known as Twin Palms Estates) and it is located directly behind the hotel. This section of Palm Springs had little development at the time and was considered away from the action downtown. The Alexanders wanted to attract people to the area, and a hotel with a fine restaurant and bar would be just the ticket to introduce visitors and hopefully new homebuyers to this up-and-coming district. They engaged William Krisel (already at work as architect on the new homes) to design the hotel. The architecture of the hotel and homes did share certain design elements, giving the whole development a cohesive, seamless look. It is with Ocotillo and Twin Palms that we first see Krisel fully utilizing his Midcentury Modern architectural language. With these projects the Alexanders gave him free rein, and he produced designs of cutting-edge architecture.

Krisel was not unfamiliar with hotels in the desert. While an architecture student at USC, he conceived of a desert hotel as a class project, which he called Mecca. In 1948, during his internship at the office of architect Paul Laszlo,

he designed and completed preliminary renderings for a hotel project that Laszlo was planning to build in La Quinta. The hotel was influenced by his USC student project and was called the Desert Comber's Club. There are distinct similarities between the unbuilt Desert Comber's Club and Ocotillo Lodge. In particular, in the Desert Comber's design there is a well-defined porte cochere in front of the main lobby, which is flanked by two-story hotel wings on either side. A keyhole-shaped pool is located directly behind the lobby building, with bungalows spread out in the area around and behind the pool.

For Ocotillo Lodge, several schemes were worked on before the final concept was selected. There was a wonderful design that featured a double-folded plate roof as a porte cochere. Another concept had the bar area hovering above the swimming pool. Different names were considered before Ocotillo Lodge was decided upon, including Sundial, Sun Flower, Desert Holiday House, and Smoke Tree Valley Club, and for each one Krisel designed a logo and typeface. The desert plant ocotillo (commonly known as candlewood) is a thin, elegant plant whose tips bloom a brilliant red. The plant provided

PLAN OF SALES OFFICE
1/4" = 1'-0"

PLOT & ROOF PLAN
1/8" = 1'-0"

project sales office

PALM SPRINGS, CALIF.

PERSPECTIVE SKETCH

PALMER & KRISEL A.I.A.

OWNER: GEORGE ALEXANDER CO.
8462 SUNSET BLVD.
HOLLYWOOD, CALIF.

architects and engineers

11757 San Vicente Boulevard / Los Angeles 49, California

GRanite 9-2129   BRadshaw 2-2055

TITLE:
PRELIMINARY STUDY
SALES OFFICE
PALM SPRINGS

Facing: Lobby and entry of Ocotillo Lodge, Palm Springs, California (circa 1957).

Right, top: View of Ocotillo Lodge with porte cochere, Palm Springs, California (circa 1957), showing the ocotillo plant (commonly known as candlewood) in the foreground.

Right, below: Early photograph of Ocotillo Lodge in the newly developing south end of Palm Springs, California (circa 1957).

OCOTILLO LODGE

IN PALM SPRIN[G]

A MAGNIFICENT NEW CONC[E]

IN ALL-YEAR DESERT LIVI[NG]

Early sales brochure cover graphic for Ocotillo Lodge—detail.

Gift of William and Corinne Krisel.
William Krisel Architectural Archive,
Getty Research Institute, Los Angeles
(2009.M.23). © J. Paul Getty Trust.

the perfect inspiration and iconography for the graphic illustrations that would adorn brochures, advertisements, matchbooks, and napkins. Krisel would also design the font that was used for the hotel signage and on the original advertising brochures.

Ocotillo Lodge featured many of the architectural elements that would be used in the adjacent Twin Palms tract homes. Such things as post-and-beam construction, which allowed for open beam ceilings where the beams extended into long exterior overhangs, dramatically expressed the architecture of the buildings. Tongue-and-groove ceilings, trellised and solid sun flap structures hanging off the beams, and walls of glass with sliding doors were prominently featured in the efficiently designed units. The bathrooms, by necessity relegated to the inside of the floor plan, featured skylights over the sink/vanity areas, so that these spaces were flooded with natural light. The indoor/outdoor feeling was prominently featured at Ocotillo Lodge, as it was in the adjacent homes. Concrete block walls provided a counterbalance to the delicate glass, so that the units felt substantial yet full of light.

Ocotillo Lodge offered both standard hotel units in the two-story wings and a time-share option in the "villa" (bungalow) units arranged around the pool. These larger-than-average villas featured a kitchen, snack bar, dressing room, and living room, with a wall of glass that opened up to a private patio. The bedroom could be sectioned off from the living area by Modernfold accordion doors, making these very comfortable suites.

At street side was a low-slung porte cochere that led into the lobby of the new hotel, where there was a reception area, shops, and administrative offices. Beyond was a dramatic central structure that curved around and floated above the swimming pool. This was the hotel restaurant and cocktail lounge called the Candlewood Room. Here, massive walls of glass, which featured a solid sun flap element for shade, curved from end to end, allowing guests and diners to view the activity in the pool below while taking in the dramatic mountainscape beyond. The Candlewood Room was advertised as one of the most beautiful rooms in America.

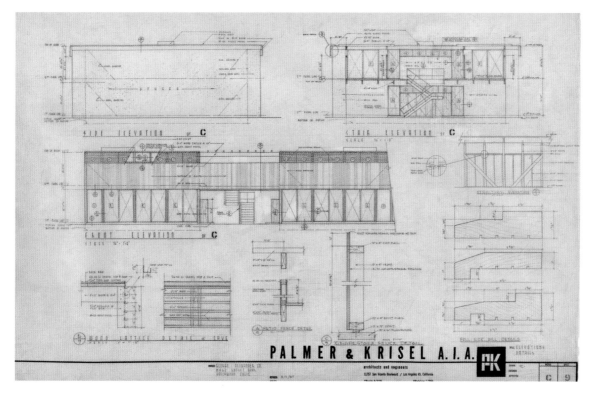

Elevation details showing original features such as sun flaps, a trellis structure in front of the clerestory windows, and T111 plywood siding (1957).

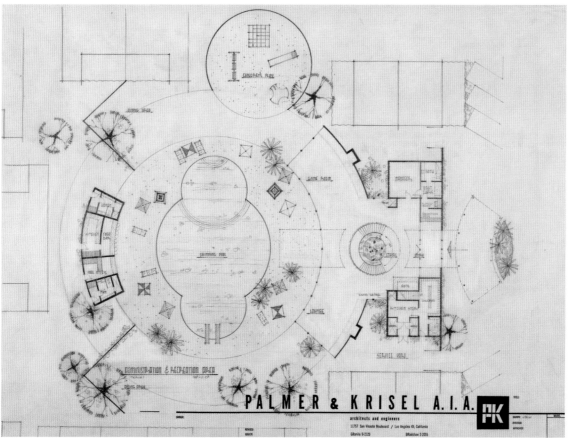

An early concept drawing of the Ocotillo Lodge public areas and pool (1955–57). Note the landscape details.

Interior of a typical accommodation at Ocotillo
Lodge (1957). For privacy, the bedroom could
be separated from the living room by a retractable
accordion-style wall.

Maynard L. Parker, photographer. Courtesy of
the Huntington Library, San Marino, California.

Ocotillo Lodge bathrooms
featured color schemes of
pumpkin, charcoal, or blue
(1957).

Maynard L. Parker, photographer.
Courtesy of the Huntington Library,
San Marino, California.

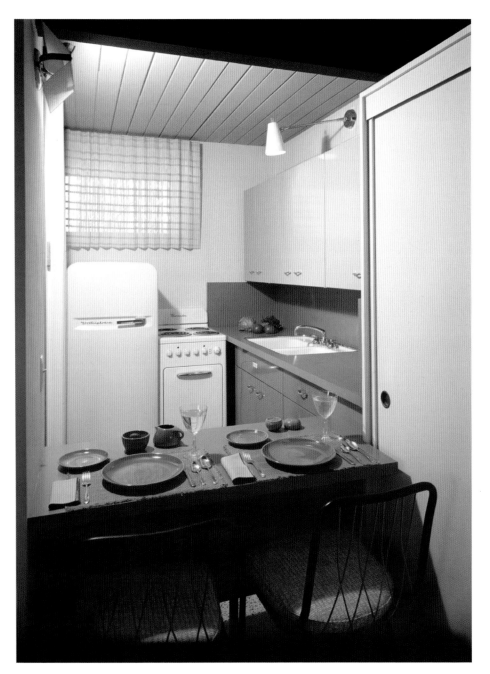

Left: Ocotillo Lodge kitchens were compact, efficient, and color-keyed to the unit (1957).

Maynard L. Parker, photographer. Courtesy of the Huntington Library, San Marino, California.

Above: Floor plan of Ocotillo Lodge bungalow, showing placement of furniture (1957).

Gift of William and Corinne Krisel. William Krisel Architectural Archive, Getty Research Institute, Los Angeles (2009.M.23). © J. Paul Getty Trust.

Facing: The interior of an Ocotillo Lodge bungalow showing a view to the bedroom, Palm Springs, California (2015).

Photograph © Darren Bradley.

Floor plan for Ocotillo Lodge showing the public rooms—the lobby, kitchen, and restaurant/bar (1957). Note that the swimming pool is different as built.

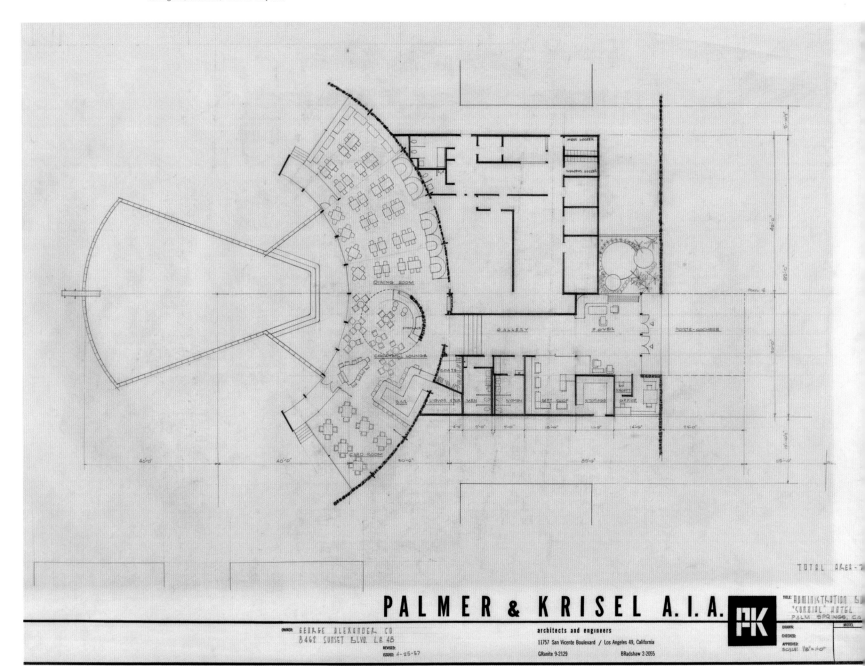

William Krisel drew several concept renderings of the interior of this restaurant and bar space, which were so elegant in their design and proportion that Bob Alexander specified that the room was to be furnished and finished exactly as in these renderings. A comparison of the renderings and subsequent photographs of the finished room shows how faithful the Alexanders were to Krisel's vision. The room featured a suspended circular ceiling that held both air conditioners and lighting and seemed to hover over the grand piano at the center. Eames shell chairs were used in the cocktail lounge, where a large open fireplace echoed the rounded form in the ceiling. Ben Dimsdale, who operated the elegant Windsor restaurant in Los Angeles, ran the Candlewood Room. (The Windsor is now a Korean restaurant called The Prince.) Persuading Dimsdale to open his restaurant here proclaimed that the Twin Palms subdivision would express the upscale lifestyle sought by potential homebuyers, and both the restaurant and lodge became an immediate success.

The swimming pool has been described as being shaped like a keyhole or champagne cork, and is still one of the largest in Palm Springs, measuring 80 by 40 feet. Garrett Eckbo, who was Krisel's landscape architecture teacher at USC, was selected by Krisel to design the landscaping. Color was important in Krisel's buildings, as it helped to express structure and material. At Ocotillo Lodge, burnt orange was used for all of the steel beams at the porte cochere and curved restaurant wall, as well as steel stair elements throughout the complex. (Steel was often delivered from the foundry primed in a rustproof orange color, making this an appropriate and associative color.) The massive textured block wing walls to either side of the porte cochere and restaurant were done in charcoal, while the main building was done in a pale tan called raffia with off-white trellis-style sun flaps that hung in front of the upper-floor windows. These are now missing.

The villas were painted various colors, from sky blue to cactus green to off-white, with beams of weathered brown or orange. This helped create individuality in the fairly dense arrangement of apartments. Interiors of the villas had four different color schemes. Similar colors were used in the Twin Palms tract homes just behind the lodge, visually linking the two projects.

Krisel also designed a temporary sales office structure adjacent to the hotel. It featured a small swimming pool behind the building. Done in a similar post-and-beam design, it and the pool conveyed the indoor/outdoor feeling that a buyer would have in one of the Twin Palms homes. After the homes sold out, the small pool was retained, while four of the nearby hotel units, two up and two down, were combined to make a large apartment for Mr. and Mrs. George Alexander. At the same time, Bob Alexander, his wife, Helene, and their daughter, Jill, took up residence in one of the now-famous butterfly-roof homes located in the new development and just around the corner from the lodge.

The hotel was so successful that the Alexanders sold it nearly a year later to Doric Motor Hotels of Seattle, Washington. The Alexanders doubled their money on the sale and put the profits to good use, as they then proceeded to develop more Midcentury Modern–style housing, much of it designed by Krisel. In 1966, actor Gene Autry acquired the hotel. Autry later sold it to Los Angeles Lakers owner Jerry Buss. In the early 1980s an investment group in Los Angeles purchased the hotel and converted all of the units into individual condominiums. During the conversion, the group attempted a minor facelift by applying elements not in harmony with the simple Midcentury Modern forms. The current homeowners association has come to recognize the beauty and importance of the architectural heritage of Ocotillo Lodge, and have a program in place to restore the structures to their originally intended look.

Rendering of the Ocotillo Lodge porte cochere,
with the lobby beyond (1955–57).

Presentation rendering of the Candlewood Room
and bar at Ocotillo Lodge (1955–57)—detail.
Note the similarity to the photograph of the
as-built Candlewood Room on page 80.

Left: The bar area in the Candlewood Room, hovering above the pool, with a view of the mountains beyond (1957).

Maynard L. Parker, photographer. Courtesy of the Huntington Library, San Marino, California.

Above: Photograph of the piano lounge in Ocotillo Lodge's Candlewood Room (1957).

Maynard L. Parker, photographer. Courtesy of the Huntington Library, San Marino, California.

Above: The swimming pool at Ocotillo Lodge (2015).

Facing: An exterior view of an Ocotillo Lodge bungalow showing the patio, Palm Springs, California (2015).

Photographs © Darren Bradley.

Ocotillo Lodge today (2015).

Photograph © Darren Bradley.

5 sandpiper

JIM WEST

Rendering of Sandpiper pool, Palm Desert, California (circa 1958). It reveals that Krisel planned to incorporate color into the overall design.

West-Prinzmetal Architectural Archives, Palm Desert, California.

"One of architecture's great challenges is to solve complex problems and then make it look easy and obvious."

— **WILLIAM KRISEL, E-MAIL TO HEIDI CREIGHTON (2015)**

Facing: Sales brochure for the Sandpiper, Palm Desert, California (1965).

West-Prinzmetal Architectural Archives, Palm Desert, California.

The Sandpiper is considered one of William Krisel's masterpieces. It is one of the best remaining examples of a concentration of Desert Modernist architecture in the Coachella Valley. Although it is frequently referred to in the singular, there are actually nine separate real estate subdivisions representing eleven building stages that occurred over a twelve-year period between 1958 and 1969. This time span makes the Sandpiper a very unique and historic landmark, as ultimately it served as a true "design and build" laboratory. One can actually see how over time the architect and builders responded to the changing needs of homeowners, the availability of building materials, and the current economy in producing a modern product that would successfully celebrate life in the desert.

View of landscaping at the Sandpiper, Palm Desert, California (circa 1958), for which Krisel received a Landscaping Merit Award. Sidewalks that transverse the site are very geometric and often match the angles of the house beams and wall protrusions.

For owners and visitors alike, the Sandpiper has often been referred to as a magical place. This magic is a product of good, *total* Krisel design. Owners with all types of interests and backgrounds generally fall for the simplicity of the architecture only to learn over time how truly sophisticated the design really is. The Sandpiper continues to be a perfect example of a design that allows one to live *large* in a smaller space. In addition, the connected common areas provide grand vistas and result in a wonderful sense of community.

THE EARLY YEARS (1958–60)

In 1958, near the corner of Highway 74 and El Paseo there was a fire station, a few smoke trees, a handful of distant houses, and a *lot of sand*. On March 2, the Western Land and Capital Company announced that this site in Palm Desert was to be developed incorporating completely new ideas in luxury desert living. The development, which would come to be known as the Sandpiper, initially started as a cooperative and ultimately became one of the first condominium projects designed and built in the Coachella Valley. The official name of the first circle of apartment units was Palm Springs Garden Apartments #1.

The builder selected for the project was George M. Holstein and Sons, which had offices in Costa Mesa, Las Vegas, and Beverly Hills. They had recently finished the Fairway Cottages at the Thunderbird Country Club. The Holstein organization was known for building high-end custom homes for many of Hollywood's most noted personalities.

View of triplex unit, Sandpiper, Palm Desert, California, with
underground utilities and early landscaping (circa 1958).

Photograph by Julius Shulman. Getty Research Institute,
Los Angeles (2004.R.10). © J. Paul Getty Trust.

View of duplex unit in Circle 7, Sandpiper,
Palm Desert, California (circa 1962–63).

A view of the Shadowal decorative concrete block wall at the Sandpiper, Palm Desert, California (circa 1958). It also shows the original exterior colors.

These were conceived as seasonal second homes and advertised as "own your own luxury garden apartments." The idea was to provide residential privacy along with resort hotel service. Such things as monogrammed Sandpiper towels, linens, gardeners, maids, and room service were to be included. A barbecue and sheltered entertaining area would be built. Recreation would include private putting greens and heated swimming pools with diving boards. The first apartments were planned at close to 1,000 square feet.

The Sandpiper project started with a survey of the property, and numerous versions of site plot plans were then developed. The chosen design incorporated eight three-unit, single-story, pinwheel-shaped buildings clustered around a common area. The typical front porch in each unit was moved to the poolside, away from the street. This configuration provided for individual privacy, as well as wonderful views of the pool "oasis," common property, sky, and nearby mountains. One must actually leave the exterior connecting roads and enter the circle in order to realize the success of this disciplined design effort.

Decorative concrete block walls were used extensively. The blocks had sculpted patterns and cutouts, and were sometimes indented for further effect when placed. Palmer & Krisel actively configured the detailed placement of many of these patterns for the Sandpiper. The Superlite Concrete Block Company of Calipatria (in the Salton Sea area) supplied the newly designed block, which was named Shadowal.

Flat roofs were used along with post-and-beam construction, which allowed the use of windows with aluminum sash, clerestory windows, and large, expansive Trimview sliding doors with Lucite handles. Construction was genuine lath and plaster. The beams and ceiling remained

The architect chosen was William Krisel of Palmer & Krisel. The firm was well respected, having received numerous national awards for their designs of homes and apartments. The firm had a reputation for being extremely practical and very conscious of builders' problems. *Progressive Architecture* listed Palmer & Krisel as one of the top one hundred firms in the nation. In this large project, Krisel was allowed to apply his skills as an architect, landscape architect, urban planner, and project manager. He also could apply the lessons learned from his involvement with the earlier Alexander projects.

Private patio with water
feature and shadow
block wall, Sandpiper,
Palm Desert, California
(circa 1962–63).

Photograph by Julius Shulman.
Getty Research Institute,
Los Angeles (2004.R.10).
© J. Paul Getty Trust.

Shadow block wall, Sandpiper, Palm Desert, California (2011).
Sandpiper designs used shadow-producing features in walls, screens,
doors, overhangs, sun flaps, terraced steps, and plantings.

Photograph © Darren Bradley.

Below: Three elevation drawings for the Sandpiper, Palm Desert, California, showing screen blocks, shadow blocks, and window and sliding door locations (1963).

West-Prinzmetal Architectural Archives, Palm Desert, California.

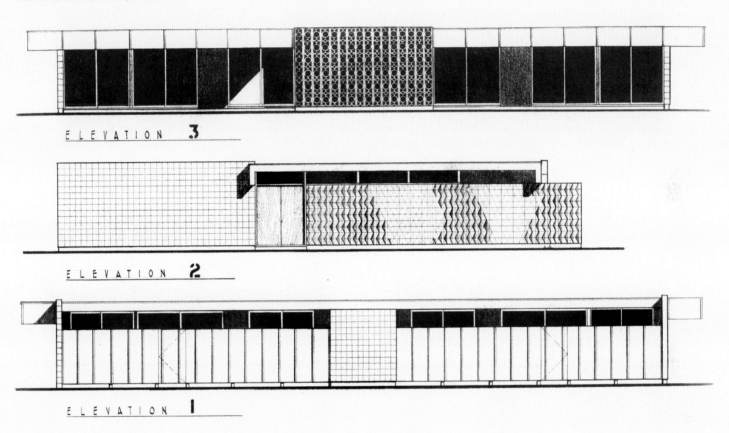

ELEVATION 3

ELEVATION 2

ELEVATION 1

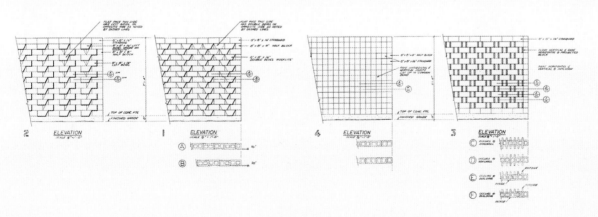

Left: Drawing of block layouts, Sandpiper, Palm Desert, California (1960).

West-Prinzmetal Architectural Archives, Palm Desert, California.

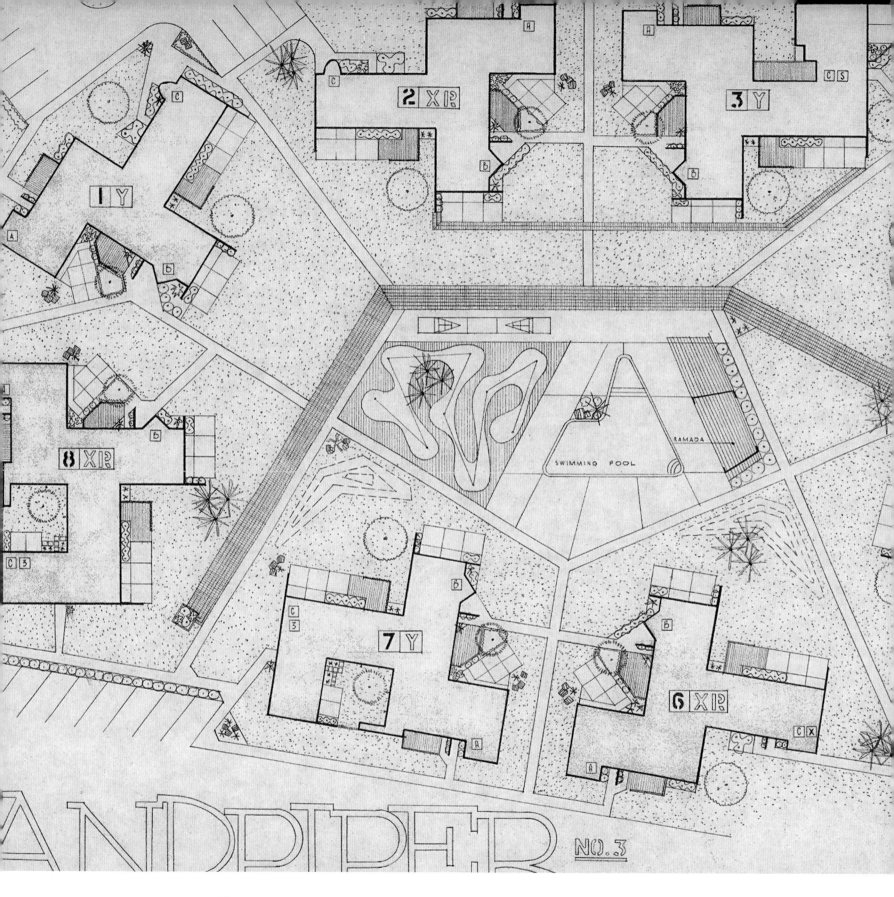

Facing: Site plan for Circle 3 at the Sandpiper, Palm Desert, California (1959). Note the detailed planning that includes building placement, elevations, terraced steps, sidewalks, patios, planters, boulders, plant material, lighting fixtures, and utilities.

West-Prinzmetal Architectural Archives, Palm Desert, California.

Below: View of the pool and ramada at the Sandpiper, Palm Desert, California (1958). The ramada was designed to provide a social meeting place where the shelter was carefully situated so that it did not block the home views.

Photograph by Julius Shulman. Getty Research Institute, Los Angeles (2004.R.10). © J. Paul Getty Trust.

View of creative hardscape at the
Sandpiper, Palm Desert, California
(circa 1958).

exposed as a design feature. The homes also included patio overhangs and a system of sun flaps that protected each unit from direct sun. Every inch of space was designed for living, storage, and relaxation. The masonry walls provided a soundproofing effect.

Krisel, who is also a landscape architect, selected all of the plants and trees and detailed their placement for the project. Careful review of the elevations resulted in the conclusion that concrete block steps could be used to help maintain the contour of the property. This allowed for drainage control, better views, and a lower building cost due to easier site preparation. The straight lines and the sharp geometric angles of the landscaping, steps, and walkways for the Sandpiper project contrasted with the rolling mountain backdrop. Krisel received a Landscaping Merit Award for the Sandpiper project.

Considerable thought was put into the shape and placement of the pool. Dramatic angles were included with the pool and ramada to provide interest and emphasize the modern aspect of the project. The common recreation area was set a few steps below grade. Each home in the three-unit buildings was creatively designed to appear unique.

View of units in Circle 7 and the geometric-shaped hardscape, Sandpiper, Palm Desert, California (circa 1962).

THE SHAPE OF TOMORROW
at the **SANDPIPER** today!

Compact . . . beautiful . . . fully automatic . . . your Sandpiper built-in kitchen exemplifies "the shape of tomorrow" by Westinghouse. The built-in range and oven make meal preparation a push-button operation, and the four-burner range top and beautiful color matched oven are the identical appliances you'd expect to find in the finest luxury home. There's plenty of refrigerator space too . . . a big Westinghouse eleven foot freezer-refrigerator with abundant storage and separate freezer chest with ice cube tray!

Either round or angled kitchens were available in the first circle. Ceiling height was varied. Block patterns were changed. Decorative exterior block walls had different heights and angles. Patios were different shapes. Buildings were reversed in orientation. Yet every owner had privacy and a view.

Krisel convinced Holstein to keep all utilities underground. Each two-bedroom, two-bath home included custom lighting fixtures by Lightrend, flexible room dividers, and modern furnishings. These were *modern* homes with all the advantages of technology: full refrigeration; color-matched electric range, oven, and refrigerator by Westinghouse; and a "Super Hush" Waste King garbage disposal. (Krisel had to include a drawing of how to install such a new thing as a garbage disposal.) Each of the early Sandpipers included a small circular marker embedded in the front doorstep entrance that read, "GOLD MEDALLION HOME—LIVE BETTER ELECTRICALLY." Desert colors were repeated in the paints, structural materials, and plantings. Many of the homes in the original first circle also included brightly colored accent walls, which extended from the interior to the exterior as well as on the sun flaps.

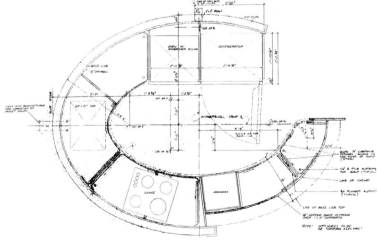

Left: Plan for the round kitchen at the Sandpiper (circa 1958).

West-Prinzmetal Architectural Archives, Palm Desert, California.

Above: View of a round kitchen designed for Sandpiper Circle 1 units, Palm Desert, California (1958). Note the segmented and retractable cabinet doors and the efficient layout.

Photograph by Julius Shulman. Getty Research Institute, Los Angeles (2004.R.10). © J. Paul Getty Trust.

Krisel would travel to the desert once a week during the construction to observe the Sandpiper project. Typically he would leave Los Angeles early in the morning and arrive in Palm Springs to first meet and have breakfast with Bob Alexander. They would review the progress of the Alexander homes projects. In the afternoon, Krisel would then travel on to Palm Desert to the Sandpiper project. These progress observation visits put Krisel in contact with all of the main elements of project construction and landscaping. His observations were not only the basis for payment of work performed but also a check on conformance to the design drawings/specifications. At the end of the day he would travel on Highway 74 to San Diego, where he would manage other projects the rest of the week.

Construction of the Sandpiper was mainly accomplished in the summer months. First, the site was cleared of large rocks that were saved for later use in the landscaping.

Krisel walked the site and adjusted the placement of each unit for maximum views. After the site elevations and common utilities were set, the four-inch floor slabs were poured. Next, the reinforced block walls were erected and the large support beams were placed. The beams were painted a dark weathered brown (using Dunn-Edwards paint) prior to their placement to support the roof. The cabinets, with smart Lucite pulls, were individually designed for each type of kitchen.

Vee Nisley of Rancho Mirage was the decorator for the model units. She introduced bright-colored modern furniture as well as accent wallpaper, mosaics, imported prints, paintings, and hanging wall sculptures. Her interior decorating emphasized the Sandpiper theme of carefree desert living. She referred to the trim customized kitchen as a "conversation kitchen . . . that was much desired in intimate desert living. . . . [T]he dining bar serves a dual

Interior of a unit at the Sandpiper, Palm Desert, California (circa 1958).
Modern and low-sitting furniture resulted in the homeowners having
spectacular pool and mountain views through the walls of sliding glass.
The design also allowed for airflow through the house from the outside.

Early rendering of
an apartment at
the Sandpiper,
Palm Desert, California
(circa 1958).

Gift of William and Corinne Krisel.
William Krisel Architectural Archive,
Getty Research Institute,
Los Angeles (2009.M.23).
© J. Paul Getty Trust.

purpose when utilized during the cocktail hour." She included furniture that would allow the effective use of the Krisel-designed flexible room divider. The owner could then switch between having a second bedroom or an extended living/den area. She also emphasized the use of the outdoor patios as additional rooms for living. Nisley was so successful in her decorating that she continued on for years decorating Sandpiper homes for new buyers.

The world-renowned architectural historian and photographer Julius Shulman took several early photographs of the Sandpiper. He made trips to the Sandpiper project during various building phases. His photographs brilliantly captured the realized Krisel vision of a man-made development fitting into the natural environment. These images appeared in numerous local and national magazines as well as in promotional literature. Shulman often used the Sandpiper as a positive example of good development in his many lectures across the world and commentaries on urban planning.

Krisel designed a Sandpiper sales office and placed it on a temporary foundation near the corner of El Paseo and Highway 74. Many years later this simple building would serve as the first location of the Palm Desert City Hall when the city incorporated in 1973.

Homes started selling at $17,995, with the last one in the first circle selling for $19,000. For the time this was a high price for a unit of this size. The homes, however, included high-end materials and appliances, and even the luxury of two bathrooms. Owners were also granted membership in the nearby Shadow Mountain Club.

"Despite the so-called recession, 123 degrees of desert heat, the wrong season . . . Sandpiper now in construction in Palm Desert is entirely sold out."
—*LOS ANGELES TIMES*, OCTOBER 1958

In the January 1959 issue of *Concrete Masonry Age* it was declared that Palmer & Krisel were the most influential architects in the United States today. The entire issue was dedicated to the firm, and included numerous Sandpiper photographs taken by Julius Shulman along with his editorial comments. Coverage of the Sandpiper

The January 1959 issue
of *Concrete Masonry Age*.

West-Prinzmetal Architectural
Archives, Palm Desert, California.

Rendering of a Model E unit at the Sandpiper, Palm Desert,
California, viewed from the interior patio (circa 1963).

View of a Sandpiper unit (2012). All homes were designed with a direct view to the pool. This discipline resulted in the added benefit of giving swimmers a view back from the pool at the surrounding architecture, especially striking in the evening when the homes reveal themselves as a circle of "architectural lanterns."

Photograph by James Schnepf/Palm Springs Modern Living.

Right: Drawing for a Model A unit, Sandpiper, Palm Desert, California, showing the courtyard landscape plan (circa 1962).

West-Prinzmetal Architectural Archives, Palm Desert, California.

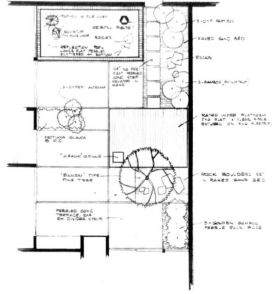

"A" PLAN COURTYARD LANDSCAPING

Rendering of a Sandpiper-type
ramada (circa 1960)—detail.

West-Prinzmetal Architectural Archives,
Palm Desert, California.

"If you have ever dreamed of a luxury home in a choice year 'round vacation land . . . but without the cost and care of upkeep? Then the Sandpiper is for you! Here, in the heart of California's desert playland Palm Desert—has been created the ultimate in a luxury cooperative residence. A home with every privacy, every facility from beautiful garden-patio to built-in kitchen . . . and combined with the finest in resort hotel service and maintenance. Yes, the Sandpiper has been created for you and can be yours without a care in the world!"

— **PROMOTIONAL SALES COPY FROM BUILDER GEORGE M. HOLSTEIN'S WESTERN LAND AND CAPITAL COMPANY (CIRCA 1958–59)**

This Sandpiper-type rendering illustrates Krisel's attention to detail, including interior views and the initials "WK" in the poolside planter (circa 1962–65).

West-Prinzmetal Architectural Archives, Palm Desert, California.

"A Kitchen should be Designed for Effortless Cooking . . . and be Sociable. The Sandpiper kitchen, by being centrally located, offers efficiency and the feeling that it loves company. The Formica counter tops are an impressive work surface. The many cabinets are custom finished and have magnetic catches. . . . The Bath: Spacious and flower fresh. Sandpiper designing accomplishes what many women search for: an atmosphere that this home is cared for. The bath reflects this view in a most individual way. A skylight offers natural lighting. Tile shower is completely enclosed in safety glass. The sunken tile tub is stunning and luxurious . . . Bedrooms should have a fresh glow that welcomes you quietly whatever the hour. With this intent, Sandpiper bedrooms effect a cool, quiet spaciousness. Dressing rooms just a tip-toe off the master bedroom, offer wall-to-wall mirrors and a skylight for natural lighting." — **FROM A DUNLIN CORPORATION BROCHURE (CIRCA 1965)**

and advertisements also appeared in the *Desert Sun, Palm Springs Life, Los Angeles Times, Shadow Mountain Club Sun Spots, House and Home,* and several other national trade publications.

This extensive media coverage influenced several other architects and builders to begin to adopt some of the concepts and materials used in the Sandpiper. Holstein had Krisel develop site plans for property he owned in Rancho Mirage near Tamarisk Country Club, applying a "Sandpiper" format to six cooperatives with pools in the middle and a similar road pattern.

At this point the Sandpiper had no exterior perimeter walls, and there were no nearby stores or malls. El Paseo east and west of Highway 74 was largely vacant. For the original owners, the Sandpiper provided a resort-like place to escape the pressures of everyday life. They would lounge in this carefree environment or venture out to find a restaurant or play in such destinations as the nearby Shadow Mountain Club.

The first circle was considered a success, and it was decided to continue the project but without the original plans for tennis courts and child play areas. A few carports were added, one of which was enclosed and used as a maid's and housekeeper's quarters as well as for linen storage in an effort to deliver on the advertised promise of "carefree living."

Circle 2 incorporated the same basic ideas, with apartments now selling for $21,500. In this circle a slightly larger pullman kitchen was added as an additional option. A variety of cutout wooden privacy screens were also installed over some of the windows. In order to fit naturally in the site, this became a more circular cluster. The ramada was made curved and the pool deck area was round with a keyhole-shaped pool similar to the one at the Krisel-designed Ocotillo Lodge.

Circle 3 is located on the highest elevation of the Sandpiper property. This larger-sized circle featured an angular pool, ramada, putting greens, large boulders, and the first Sandpiper shuffleboard court. Some owners were original owners in Circle 1 and were friends of George Holstein. Additional rooms were included, select bathrooms were made more deluxe, and large-sized enclosed patios were added. Many of the new features developed in this circle were used in later Sandpiper designs. Promotional photographs of this circle were used in advertisements to sell later Sandpipers. These ads showed maids standing at attention around the pool while happy owners lounged or practiced their putting game.

> "To WINTER in the desert playground of the Palm Springs area has been the dream of all who know California. Now this dream can come true in a simple and interesting manner. On the highway at Palm Desert, midway between Palm Springs and Indio, is The Sandpiper—the ultimate in desert living . . . these luxury homes, built on an own-your-own basis are now well into their fourth cluster. They provide every privacy and every facility from beautiful enclosed patio gardens to built-in electric kitchens— all combined with the finest in resort hotel service and maintenance. Without a care in the world one may revel in desert sunshine, invigorating clear air, in interesting mountains and wide stretches of golden sand." —*PICTORIAL CALIFORNIA,* 1960

Circle 4 represented the start of a westerly expansion. Apartments were now selling for $22,500. The ramada was designed in a triangular shape and was neatly placed into the landscape. Many of the Sandpiper owners by now were coming from Southern California and using their units as weekend getaways. The Sandpiper was no longer limited to winter use as originally conceived.

THE MIDDLE YEARS (1961–65)

Krisel designed Canyon View Estates (1961–63) in Palm Springs for the builder Roy Fey, incorporating many of the ideas developed in the early Palm Desert Sandpipers.

During this same period, George Osborn and William Kemp (both Sandpiper homeowners themselves), operating under the title of Sandpiper Builders, Inc., took over the mission of completing the remainder of the Sandpiper project. Kemp and Osborn felt that people would be willing to spend more money on larger Sandpiper units that could be designed to better accommodate guests. Krisel made the switch to clusters of eight single-story buildings, each containing two apartments. All the remaining Sandpipers would now be built as condominiums, with each buyer getting a deed to the land immediately under the apartment and an undivided interest in the common area of the circle of homes. This was a new concept at the time. The original four Sandpiper cooperative circles would eventually convert to condominiums. Over the next five years, new Sandpiper circles would have sixteen homes per circle and range in size from 1,300 to over 2,175 square feet.

The ceilings were of multiple heights and no longer had exposed beams. In addition to features found in the earlier Sandpipers, all units offered both front and rear entry and included their own laundry facilities. Buildings had less exposed wood on the exterior. There was now copper plumbing and the appliance brand of choice was Frigidaire. Day and Night Air Conditioning and Heating provided climate control. Custom Schlage front door fixtures and door

pulls were used along with distinctive door patterns. There were double-case washbasins, wall-to-wall wardrobes, Moen faucets, wet bars, acoustical ceilings, Formica-topped pullmans and counters, celestial glass, and large entry areas. All overhead lighting fixtures inside and over the patios were now recessed. Cabinets throughout the units were of a higher quality.

Krisel continued to pay strict attention to the importance of site lines to both the pool and the mountains, as he felt that those views were a major design criterion. He made extensive use of shadow blocks and screen blocks in his designs. The ramada no longer was designed with a step up and terrazzo, but rather with a single concrete surface extending out to the pool deck. More carports were now incorporated into the site plan as homes were now routinely being used for months at a time.

During this period of construction, on a visit to Bing Crosby's house located in nearby Silver Spur Ranch, President Kennedy traveled down El Paseo past the Sandpiper, resulting in increased media coverage of the area. Another positive impact on the area was the construction of the nearby College of the Desert in 1961. And around the same time, scenes from the movie *It's a Mad, Mad, Mad, Mad World* were filmed on Highway 74 south of the Sandpiper, continuing the close tradition of connections between the entertainment industry and Palm Desert. In order to meet increasing demands for additional Sandpiper units, spurred in part by this increased awareness of Palm Desert as a resort destination, Krisel designed a new sales office for Sandpiper Builders, Inc., located on El Paseo.

Krisel was asked to design Sandpiper circles to be built in Indian Wells near the Indian Wells Country Club by Sandpiper Builders, Inc. He also developed proposals for projects in La Quinta.

Street view of a Sandpiper unit built in 1959, Palm Desert, California (2012). These units featured both a private patio—in this case on the right side and enclosed by block walls off the master bedroom—and a more public patio off the living room, facing the pool.

Photograph by James Schnepf/*Palm Springs Modern Living*.

In 1964, Sandpiper prices ranged from $30,000 to $42,000. The Sandpiper project was included in the Homes for Better Living Program sponsored by the American Institute of Architects in cooperation with the magazines *House and Home* and *The American Home*.

In 2010, Sandpiper Circles 11 and 12 were the first to emphasize a low-water landscape. They also were the first circles for which an application was made to the City of Palm Desert to be considered as a historic district.

THE LATER YEARS (1966–69)

In 1967, Krisel designed the Kings Point Condominiums in Palm Springs for builder Robert Grundt. These designs reflect many of the features and materials found in the units built in the middle years of the Palm Desert Sandpiper project.

In 1968, Krisel designed the Canyon Lake development in Riverside County, California, using the Sandpiper format.

Kemp built out the remainder of the Sandpiper without the regular direct participation of Krisel. Earlier design features of the Sandpiper along with concepts from the Krisel-designed Indian Wells Sandpiper were incorporated in these last built designs.

The builder introduced some new exterior materials. A layered stone look was substituted for the standard concrete block. In addition, metal posts were used for supports on the poolside patios. In these circles, no Krisel-designed ramada structures were ever included. Several of these homes border a public street and the results are more traditional, with front lawns, individual driveways, and sidewalks to the street, as well as mailboxes and front globe pole lamps.

View from the Circle 2 pool at the Sandpiper, Palm Desert, California (2012). Circle 2 is a good example of how Krisel treated every Sandpiper building site individually. The gradually sloping property did not require concrete steps and it was more circular in shape. The site plan solution included a curved ramada, a keyhole-shaped pool, and curving sidewalks.

Photograph by James Schnepf/ *Palm Springs Modern Living.*

Home prices ranged from $36,000 to $46,000. Prices at this time did not include carpets, drapes, dining room fixtures, interior patio paving, or landscaping. This kept the selling price more competitive as development expanded in the Coachella Valley. Houses were designed to include walk-in closets and were geared towards long-term and permanent owners. Sizes ranged from 1,880 square feet to over 2,600 square feet.

In the end, the Sandpiper included 306 individual homes and eighteen swimming pools entwined with private roads and walkways spread over nearly fifty-five acres. The historic project proved that an "own your own apartment" concept would be practical to live in and financially successful to build in the desert environment.

The "modern" Sandpiper paved the way for many more developments in Palm Desert and the rest of the Coachella Valley. Many of these later projects chose materials and design features first introduced and promoted at the Krisel-designed Sandpiper.

1963 Model C house at the Sandpiper,
Palm Desert, California (2012).

Photograph by James Schnepf/*Palm Springs
Modern Living*.

condominiums

SIAN WINSHIP

"Bill [Krisel] gracefully bridged the divide between the architect and the builder to create a timeless and modern sense of residential comfort." — LEO MARMOL, FAIA

In recent years, Palm Springs preservationists have placed much emphasis on the midcentury single-family residences William Krisel designed. During the 1960s, however, condominiums played a transformational role in the evolution of the Coachella Valley desert communities from resort towns to residential communities. And Krisel was there. In fact, his architectural contributions to multifamily residential design offer a powerful case study for the architect's unique talents.

The roots of desert condominiums are found as early as 1955, when the Los Angeles Home Show featured a full-scale model exhibit for an "own-your-own cooperative apartment planned for the Palm Springs area."[1] Designed by former Palmer & Krisel partner John C. Lindsay, the apartments were presented as full-time or vacation residences that could be leased when not in use. That same year, the first cooperative, Desert Braemar, was erected near Tamarisk Country Club in Rancho Mirage.[2]

121

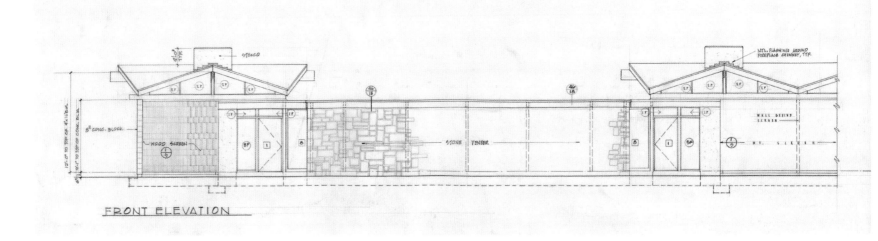

FRONT ELEVATION

Indeed, Palm Springs became the first city in California (and one of the first resorts in the nation) to legalize condominiums as a new form of vacation housing.[3] The precursor to the condominium had been the cooperative apartment. Cooperative apartments were owned collectively: owners technically owned a share or percentage of the project. Condominiums diverged from cooperative apartments in that each unit was owned individually and monthly ownership dues funded maintenance of the common areas.[4] A lack of financing for the new ownership concept, however, suppressed development until 1964. In 1961, the FHA was authorized to insure mortgages on "condos" for 85 percent of the appraised value; yet it wasn't until September 1963 that tax appraisal methods for the condominium were settled and developers began building them in full force.[5]

As desert developers shifted from single-family residences to cooperative apartments and condominiums, Palmer & Krisel followed them into the new housing types. Krisel explained the evolution of his work with developers as follows: "Historically we started with houses, then small jobs, then small apartments, then tracts and bigger apartments and then office buildings and then high rises and one thing just led to another. And we never had to solicit work."[6]

Krisel's work for George M. Holstein on the Loma Palisades project in San Diego in the mid-1950s ultimately led to

Krisel's first desert cooperative apartment commission: Sandpiper in Palm Desert (Palmer & Krisel, 1958–69). Krisel approached the design for the Sandpiper garden apartments by bringing lessons learned from tract housing design to this new form of housing. Sandpiper was a masterpiece of integrated planning, modern architecture, and landscaping.

From a planning perspective, these new forms of homeownership in the desert were rooted in the English garden city movement of the late nineteenth century, European designs for multifamily housing, and the work of Clarence S. Stein (1882–1975). Englishman Ebenezer Howard (1850–1928) is widely credited with introducing the garden city concept in his book *Garden Cities of Tomorrow* in 1902 (originally published in 1898 under the title *Tomorrow: A Peaceful Path to Real Reform*). A reaction to the unsanitary city conditions caused by capitalism and the industrial age, Howard sought to create a new community commonly owned through a limited-dividend company. The town would include the best of the country (open spaces and gardens) and the advantages of the city (intellectually stimulating activities and opportunities). Fresh air, light, open space, and gardens were essential elements of the unified plan of architectural and landscape design.

These site-planning ideas spread to the United States during the 1920s. Leading this revolution in modern

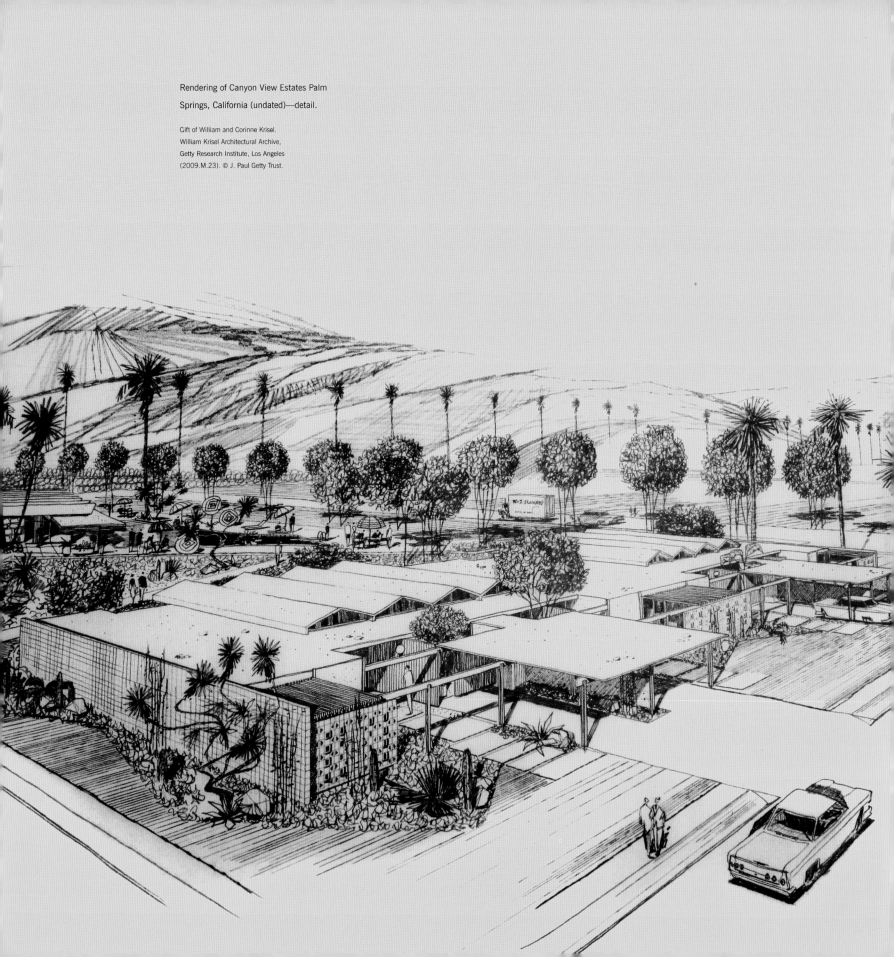

Rendering of Canyon View Estates Palm
Springs, California (undated)—detail.

housing were renowned urban planners Clarence S. Stein and Henry Wright (1878–1936). Their plan for low- to moderate-income multifamily rental housing at Radburn, New Jersey, incorporated the European superblock concept. At Radburn, a park and landscaped green space formed the backbone of the community rather than an urban grid. Houses were then turned from outside to in—placing living room windows toward the green spaces rather than the street. Stein and Wright's design for Radburn also offered the complete separation of pedestrian and automobile traffic, relegating the automobile to the periphery of the site. The net effect was a bucolic and graceful way of living that encouraged physical activity and social interaction.

Deftly adapted, these principles were translated for a graceful, luxurious, and quintessentially elegant midcentury Palm Springs lifestyle. Sandpiper's "own-your-own garden cottages" offered a new option: the best of a private residence combined with resort hotel amenities.[7]

Sandpiper stands as testimony to what a fully integrated approach to design can achieve in the hands of a master architect. However, the talent of a master architect is even better understood through the projects that face predetermined constraints or unexpected challenges along the way. Two such projects include Canyon View Estates (William Krisel, 1961–63) and Kings Point (William Krisel, 1967) in Palm Springs.

Among the early proponents of the condominium concept in Palm Springs was insurance salesman-turned-developer Roy Fey (1915–2000). Fey's niche was to sell real estate in the south end of Palm Springs to a predominantly Jewish clientele who were often barred by restrictive covenants in other areas.[8] In 1963, Fey converted his Desertaire Apartments into the Desert Skies Apartment Hotel (Claude A. Powell, 1956) and became the self-proclaimed "first person to introduce the concept of condominium building to the area."[9] Although several other Palm Springs projects were built specifically as condominiums as early as 1960, Fey was certainly an early booster for the idea. For one of his first new construction projects, Canyon View Estates, he turned to Krisel, who by this time had dissolved his long-term partnership with Dan Saxon Palmer.

Unlike Sandpiper, the site for Canyon View Estates was a small, rectangular parcel on Native American land in the south end of Palm Springs. According to Krisel, "Fey was, of course, thinking of a multi-story apartment building, but I immediately said I didn't think that was appropriate. I thought phasing from single-family homes to condos should be a gradual step where it really was a single-story building with your own individual front door and your own terrace and parking space, but there would be common recreational facilities such as swimming pools."[10]

To maximize his return on investment, Fey required higher density than Sandpiper with a saleable mix of two-bedroom and three-bedroom units. Krisel responded to the challenge with a design for twenty-eight units arranged as six four-unit buildings and two two-unit buildings around a central green space and pool. In hindsight, the plan drew upon many of Stein and Wright's successful Radburn ideas, including the landscaped backbone of the plan and complete separation of pedestrian and automobile traffic. With respect to the individual units, Krisel's post-and-beam designs for two-bedroom and three-bedroom floor plans featured living rooms and master bedrooms that opened onto private patios and visually connected with the pool and lushly landscaped recreation areas at the center of the site. Although the entrances to the units were traditionally accessed from the street, the rear elevations were effectively second entrances accessed daily as a central part of the resort lifestyle.

A gently undulating site at Canyon View Estates,
Palm Springs, California, where gable rooflines
echo views of the surrounding mountains (2015).

Photograph © Darren Bradley.

Krisel's lively designs for the concrete block walls at
Canyon View Estates, Palm Springs, California, create
texture and the play of light and shadow (2015).

Photograph © Darren Bradley.

Pop-up gable windows at Canyon View Estates, Palm Springs, California, create views and let light into the units from multiple angles, while concrete block walls provide texture for design (2015).

Photograph © Darren Bradley.

What made the design for Canyon View Estates especially effective, however, was Krisel's use of pop-up flat and gable clerestory window volumes in the central living space. This created a dynamic playfulness in section, making relatively small rooms feel generous. The windows also let light in from a multiplicity of directions and provided views of the mountains. All of this, however, was accomplished with peak construction efficiency. Clusters of mirrored plans took advantage of adjacent plumbing cores in kitchens and bathrooms and shared driveways.

Krisel's brilliance, however, was not just limited to the interior spaces. His experience in designing tract housing in the desert communities and beyond had taught him that buyers appreciated individuality in streetscapes. Indeed, the homogenization of life that had been Levittown presented even more of a threat as cooperative apartments and condominiums burst on the scene. Krisel's purposeful rotation of roofline designs and lot setbacks gave his single-family housing tract developments a dynamic visual and architectural cadence that added distinctiveness to merchant-built homes and created a unique sense of place.

At Canyon View Estates, Krisel applied that principle with two roofline treatments for his clerestory windows: the folded-plane roofline and the pop-up gable. This dynamism is clearly visible in the architect's rendering for the project featured on the cover of the marketing brochure. Moreover, the placement of the roof styles on the plot plan is not a repetitive A-B-A-B pattern, but rather a carefully considered asymmetrical composition. As a result, the streetscape along Sierra Madre Drive was very different from that seen along Sky View Drive. This practice was rarely applied in other developments. This dynamic architectural cadence was distinguished from other desert projects from the period, such as Royal Hawaiian Estates (Wexler & Harrison, 1960) or nearby Country Club Estates (Jones and Emmons,

1963–64), in which a single roofline design was consistently displayed. In particular, the Country Club Estates scheme featured identical clusters of long, low, repetitive horizontal rooflines and solid massing that lacked the dynamism of the Krisel design.

Adding to the diversity of elevations was Krisel's original design for textured concrete block walls. Krisel's desert architecture often deftly used the economic concrete masonry unit for its insulating properties as well as its ability to create a dynamic geometrical interplay between solid and void. His designs for the use of cut and carefully placed standardized blocks are a case study of the design, economy, and efficiency that made Krisel a success with builders and homeowners alike.

Unfortunately, at Canyon View Estates, Fey usurped Krisel's decision to exclusively use concrete block in favor of natural stone.[11] Fey perceived stone as a more luxurious material that could command higher sales prices. Marketed by Fey as "prestige homes for people of prestige,"[12] Canyon View Estates was successful even without mention of its architectural pedigree. "Luxurious, carefree desert living in a beautifully-designed country-like setting. Condominium living amid park-like gardens, expansive lawns and emerald putting greens."[13] The location near Canyon Country Club in the "fashionable south end"[14] was also a selling point. Fey expanded the initial development to include five additional phases on adjacent parcels. These reflected a higher concentration of the pop-up gable roofline versus the folded

Dramatic poolside or fairway elevation for Model B-1 at Kings Point, Palm Springs, California (undated)—detail.

plane, as well as stone cladding. To this day, residents of Canyon View Estates recognize the value that the superb architectural design brings to their daily living experiences.

Another Krisel condominium project worthy of study is Kings Point. Located on an irregular-shaped eleven-acre parcel jutting into the golf course at the south end of exclusive Canyon Country Club, these detached single-family residences were exceptional examples of Krisel applying his design talent to golf club residential development.

While Palm Springs had long been known as a spot for fun in the sun and active outdoor recreation, in the years following World War II, the desert became synonymous with the sport of golf.[15]

The development of Thunderbird Country Club in 1951 changed the paradigm of golf course development in the desert from an expensive, water-demanding investment to a residential real estate model where homesites were integrated into golf course design. Golf's popularity was also enabled by the development of golf carts, air conditioning, and increased media exposure from televised tournaments and the nation's leading golf enthusiast, President Dwight D. Eisenhower.

Canyon Country Club was developed in the early 1960s at a cost of $50 million. Located on Agua Caliente land, the club was the culmination of years of effort by Andrew Catapano and Harold M. Simon of Palm Canyon Country Club, Inc., to secure the site. Ultimately, the project was to be the largest Native American land lease in American history.[16]

Although the club was primarily designed as a custom home development, a small parcel along the second fairway was reserved for future development by Robert Grundt's Golf Club Sales Company, a subsidiary of his New York–based First National Realty and Construction Corporation. Subdivided in 1969, Kings Point was designed to add condominium-style living options to the Canyon Country Club offerings.

Like Sandpiper, Kings Point offered Krisel the opportunity to bring integrated planning, architecture, and landscape design to the project. The homes were sited along the edges of the V-shaped parcel for maximum fairway exposure, with the remaining units clustered internally around the pool and greenbelt area. Walkways on the diagonal, reminiscent of Sandpiper, created unusual geometries and vistas throughout the landscaped heart of the community. A tennis club and courts were sited at the southwestern end at the corner of two busy thoroughfares.

The architect's contribution to Kings Point can be seen from the project's inception. Two alternate plot plan designs survive in the Krisel archives. The first plot plan study featured a relatively even allocation between the larger, 2,734-square-foot, three-bedroom, two-and-a-half-bath Plan A, and the smaller, 2,240-square-foot, three-bedroom, two-and-a-half-bath Plan B. A later scheme (and ultimately the one built) shows how Krisel refined the plan to include more smaller Plan B units, redrew the parcel lines to better align lot size with product value, and added "reverse" plans to diversify the mix.

The final project was a forty-four-unit development consisting of two floor plans, six exterior elevations, and reversed or flopped plans where a single design appears an average of just three times throughout the complex. The net effect of this was that each home felt unique and different, and a

This street elevation for Model B-3 at Kings Point, Palm Springs, California, offers a distinctive play on solid and void (undated)—detail.

Gift of William and Corinne Krisel. William Krisel Architectural Archive, Getty Research Institute, Los Angeles (2009.M.23). © J. Paul Getty Trust.

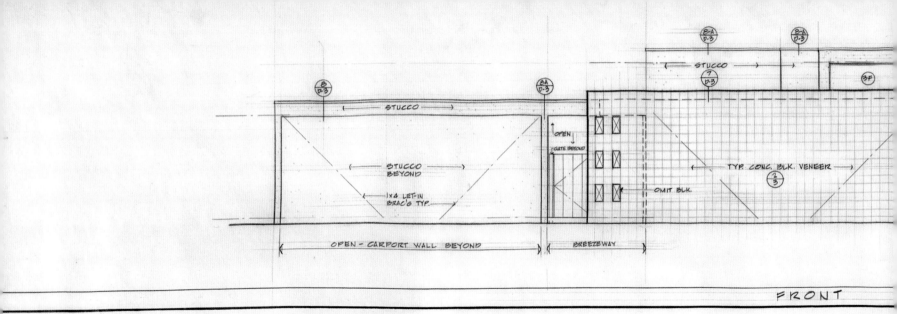

STUCCO

STUCCO
BEYOND

1x4 LET-IN
BRAC'G TYP.

OPEN
GATE BEYOND

OMIT BLK.

STUCCO

TYP. CONC. BLK. VENEER

OPEN - CARPORT WALL BEYOND

BREEZEWAY

FRONT

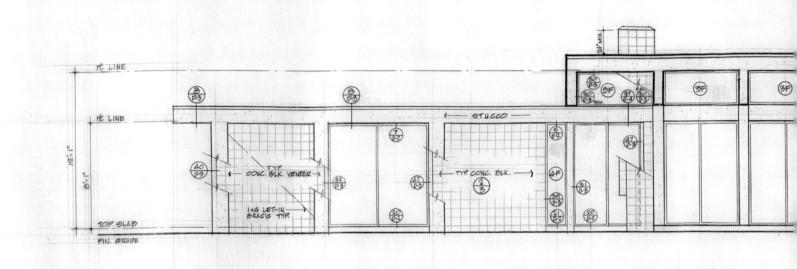

℄ LINE

℄ LINE

12'-1"

8'-1"

TOP SLAB

FIN. GRADE

STUCCO

TYP.
CONC. BLK. VENEER

1x4 LET-IN
BRAC'G TYP.

TYP CONC. BLK.

24" MIN.

REAR

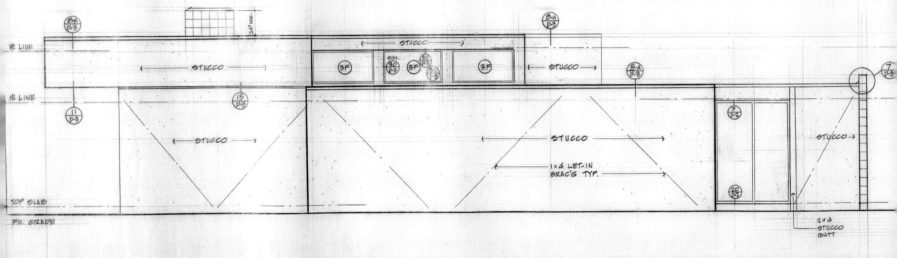

℄ LINE

℄ LINE

TOP SLAB

FIN. GRADE

STUCCO

STUCCO

STUCCO

STUCCO

STUCCO

STUCCO

1x4 LET-IN
BRAC'G TYP.

24" MIN.

1x4
STUCCO
BATT

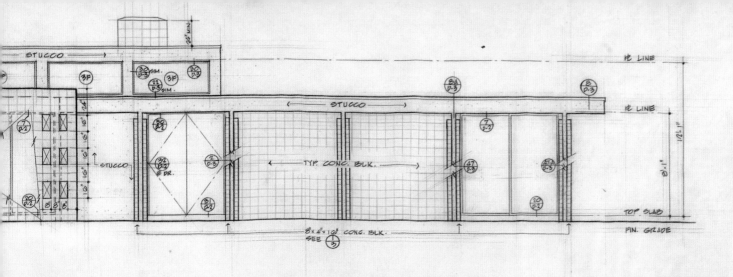

ELEVATION

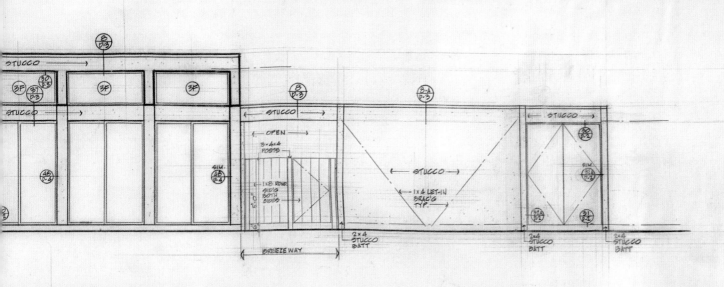

ELEVATION

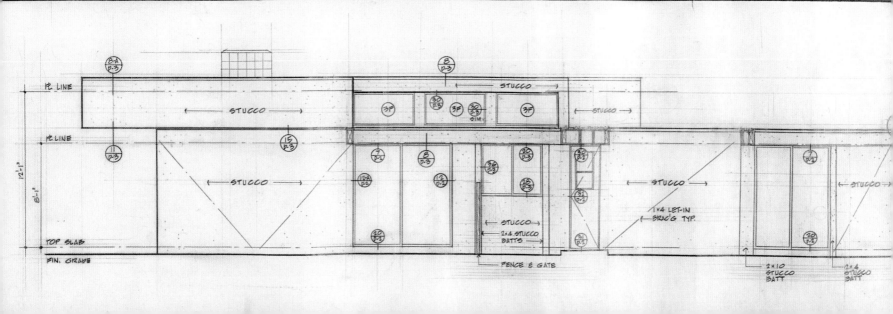

stimulating visual rhythm was created along the street-scape. Krisel's use of an alphanumeric coding system (e.g., B2R) dated back to his early postwar tract developments in Los Angeles.[17] At Kings Point, the system was in full flower—delivering the optimal mix of construction efficiency and individuality in design.

Another exceptional quality of Krisel's designs for Kings Point was the architect's acknowledgment that the homes effectively had two primary elevations: the street and the fairway. The rear fairway elevations were designed with as much aesthetic purpose as the street views. The golf course was effectively the new greenbelt for garden city living. Fairway elevations for all six designs were dramatic and dynamic in their own right, featuring floor-to-ceiling glass.

With Kings Point being a luxury condominium develop-ment, Krisel took the open plan a step beyond his other desert designs and created a spacious, stepped-down "gar-den room" at the center of the plan. This terrazzo-lined space was positioned directly under a pop-up clerestory window element. The larger Plan A also featured a luxuri-ous two-sided fireplace between the garden room and the living room. Both plans were oriented toward the fairway or pool and garden views.

At Kings Point, Krisel also demonstrated an evolved architec-tural language of Modernism. Still deftly plying the Modern tools of space and light, solid and void, Krisel's designs for Kings Point displayed an elegance, refinement, and sophis-tication that evoked Ludwig Mies van der Rohe's structural

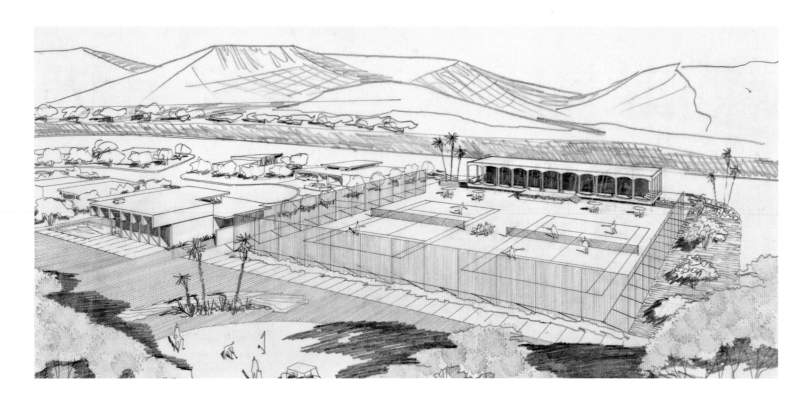

expression more than in previous Krisel designs. And while the distinctive architectural cadence of the houses from the street is undeniable, it is subtler and less exuberant than some of his earlier, more retail-oriented designs.[18]

Krisel's design for the Kings Point Tennis Club depicted a floating pavilion with an elegant tension between solid and void elements interacting at its core, however the original design was not realized. The clean, modern lines of the pavilion acted as a three-dimensional advertisement for the luxurious lifestyle for sale at Kings Point.

In addition to the on-site amenities, Kings Point residency came with access to Canyon Country Club's two eighteen-hole golf courses. Relieved of burdensome maintenance problems such as gardening and pool care, Kings Point residents were left "to enjoy the unparalleled freedom and charm unique to California's most celebrated resort—Palm Springs."[19]

In recent years, much well-deserved attention has been focused on Krisel's single-family residential tracts. Yet his contribution to multifamily residential design was undeniable. Many of the elements that identify Krisel's work—aesthetic purity, capturing light from a multiplicity of angles, connection with the short and distant vistas, privacy, a dynamic architectural cadence and sense of individuality, and efficiency in materials and construction methods—distinguished his cooperative apartment and condominium

A perspective drawing of the tennis courts and pavilion at Kings Point as viewed from South Camino Real, Palm Springs, California (undated)—detail.

Top left: Blanch Teterka at the Kings Point pool, Palm Springs, California (1972). Note the diagonal vistas along the greenbelt area towards the mountains.

Left: 2750 Kings Road East under construction, Kings Point, Palm Springs, California (1969).

Above: Completed unit at Kings Point, Palm Springs, California (1969).

Photographs courtesy of Peter Siegel and Jon Patrick.

work as well. The same elements were also present in Krisel's later work in high-rise development, where his talent in planning and siting elevated the architectural experience of more traditional apartment-style living. Two distinctive examples of this were Ocean Avenue Towers (Krisel/Shapiro & Associates, 1971) in Santa Monica and Coronado Shores (Krisel/Shapiro & Associates, 1972–78) in the San Diego area.

In 1967, the vision of the Palm Springs area as a site for vacation homeownership was given another boost when direct service to Palm Springs by transcontinental air carriers was established. Many vacationers and potential homebuyers were lured to the desert. By the 1970s, however, the minimalist lines of Midcentury Modern architecture were giving way to the shed-style Modern popularized at Sea Ranch on the Northern California coast and a return to Spanish Colonial influences. The timelessness of Krisel's Modern architecture and planning at Canyon View Estates and Kings Point is proved constantly, however, as new generations of appreciative visitors enjoy the fulfilled promise of the desert lifestyle.

NOTES

1. "A Desert Apartment," *Los Angeles Times,* June 12, 1955, 118.

2. "Co-Op Living: The New Trend in the Desert," *Palm Springs Life,* December 1960, 11–17.

3. Lawrence Culver, *The Frontier of Leisure*: Southern California and the Shaping of Modern America (New York: Oxford University Press, 2010), 193.

4. Cooperative apartments were popular in dense urban centers such as Chicago and New York.

5. Dan MacMasters, "Condominiums—The Most Exciting Housing Development in 15 Years," *Los Angeles Times,* July 26, 1964, 44.

6. John Crosse, *William Krisel Oral History* (Playa del Rey, CA: modern-ISM Press, 2009), 83.

7. Advertisement, *Desert Sun,* March 13, 1959.

8. John Stephen Edwards, Ph.D., to William Krisel, January 15, 2011. William Krisel Papers, 1935–2014, Getty Research Institute, Los Angeles. Accession no. 2009.M.23.

9. "Roy and Bob Fey: Where It Began," *Palm Springs Life,* May 1980, 55.

10. Lawrence Karol, "Quiet—and Idyllic—on the Set!" *Palm Springs Life,* July 2013. www.palmspringslife.com/Palm-Springs-Life/July-2013/Quiet-and-Idyllic-on-the-Set.

11. William Krisel, e-mail to Sian Winship, January 22, 2015.

12. "The Wonderful World of Canyon View Estates," *Palm Springs Life,* November 1965.

13. Karol, "Quiet and Idyllic On the Set."

14. "The Wonderful World of Canyon View Estates."

15. Culver, *The Frontier of Leisure,* 189.

16. "Canyon Country Club," clipping file, Palm Springs Historical Society.

17. The letter stood for the plan, the numeral for the elevation design, and the final "R" indicated the plan was the reverse of the original design.

18. Postwar homebuyers were often drawn to subdivisions on the weekends to view model homes. Competition was keen among builders and developments during this period, and differentiating one's product was often a key to success.

19. Kings Point brochure, William Krisel Papers, 1935–2014, Getty Research Institute, Los Angeles. Accession no. 2009.M.23.

Kings Point home,
Palm Springs, California
(2015).

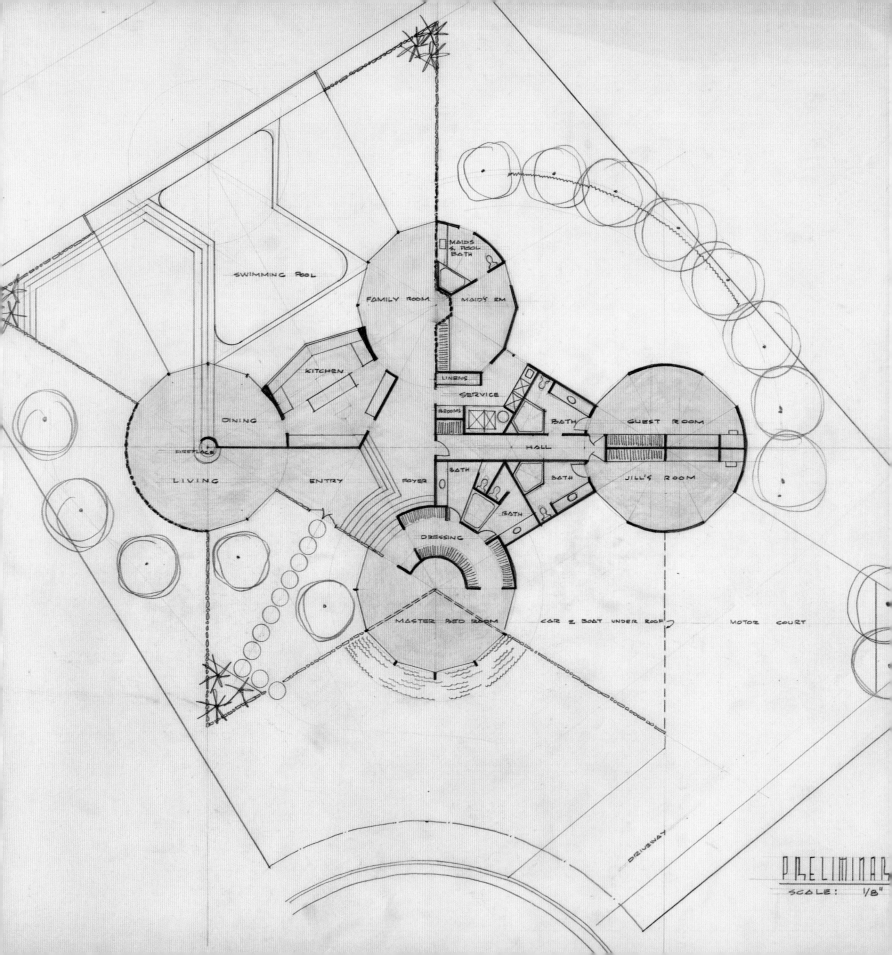

SWIMMING POOL

MAIDS & POOL BATH

FAMILY ROOM

MAID'S RM

KITCHEN

LINENS

SERVICE

A-ROOMS

BATH

GUEST ROOM

DINING

HALL

FIREPLACE

LIVING

ENTRY

FOYER

BATH

BATH

JILL'S ROOM

BATH

DRESSING

MASTER BED ROOM

CAR & BOAT UNDER ROOF

MOTOR COURT

DRIVEWAY

PRELIMINARY

SCALE: 1/8"

krisel goes custom

BARBARA LAMPRECHT

"Circles have no leading edge. You can approach them from anywhere."

— WILLIAM KRISEL, INTERVIEW WITH BARBARA LAMPRECHT (JULY 22, 2015)

Left: Kemp Residence, Palm Desert, California (2011).

Photograph by Patrick Ketchum, KetchumPhotography.com.

Three custom homes designed by William Krisel—the Alexander Residence (also known as the "House of Tomorrow") in Palm Springs (1960); the Kemp Residence (also known as the "Lost Krisel") in Palm Desert (1963); and the Tipper-Grundt Residence in Palm Springs (1968)—reflect an unusual advantage that developers of tract homes have over other builders. While the tract is being built, that developer is already familiar with the local planning department and building codes. He's developed a solid relationship with an architect who has refined a successful paradigm. He or his team has negotiated with city officials and knows the choicest sites. Other key elements such as surveyors, geologists, trusted superintendents, their subcontractors, materials sources, and even earth-moving equipment are at the ready as well.

So one thing that never surprised Bill Krisel was the virtually inevitable request from that developer to design a family home. Between 1950 and 1969, of the sixty-two custom houses he designed (fifty-five were executed, primarily in Beverly Hills, Los Angeles, Palm Springs, and San Diego), at least ten were for developers. Krisel established his voice with those custom homes, territory in which he kept innovating and developing his strategies. In turn, this custom work fueled the designs of his tract developments.

In these luxury houses, Krisel invariably applied certain of the materials and strategies that made his tract homes so light filled and easygoing. However, these three clients provided the rare opportunity not only to tackle a unique program and site but to do so on pretty much an unlimited

Facing: Preliminary floor plan for the first version of the House of Tomorrow, Vista Las Palmas, Palm Springs, California (circa 1960)—detail. Note the early landscape concept and the hourglass-shaped pool similar to that of the Ocotillo Lodge pool.

Gift of William and Corinne Krisel. William Krisel Architectural Archive, Getty Research Institute, Los Angeles (2009.M.23). © J. Paul Getty Trust.

budget. There was another difference, too. With most custom house designs, long and potentially meandering meetings with clients new to working with architects and the process of house design are part of the package. Some architects thrive on navigating that tender environment, but Krisel had grown to prefer the faster pace, larger efficiencies, and relative anonymity of tract design. However, with these three clients, all seasoned and experienced, Krisel had the best of both worlds. They knew his work, understood that good construction doesn't come cheap, and trusted his ability to deliver the exceptional. So they gave him free rein. That was defined anywhere from the intense camaraderie of private charrettes with his high-powered friend Robert (Bob) Alexander—so the developer could deliver the house as a surprise to his wife, the glamorous, effervescent Helene—to the hands-off attitude of William Kemp. Krisel never even met Kemp's wife or children; Kemp only made one suggestion (and a good one, discussed later), and Krisel performed no construction oversight. In fact, he forgot about it. He didn't see the exceptionally beautiful result now known as the "Lost Krisel" until decades later.

Nonetheless, free rein or no, each of the custom houses exhibits a sibling resemblance to their developer's own approach, reflecting Krisel's insight into that individual developer's tastes and needs. The generous clerestories that follow below a sloping roofline in some of Krisel's tract models, first developed in his custom work, are brought to a crescendo at the Alexander Residence, where they are so dramatically rendered.[1] His characteristically playful dialogue between angles and curves is here in abundance as well.

The fluid horizontality of the Sandpiper in Palm Desert, a tract of 306 condominiums purchased and finished by Kemp with his partner George Osborn, can be traced to the same early thinking that later informed the Kemp Residence's long, relaxed extensions into the landscape. By contrast,

the secluded Tipper-Grundt Residence, located on the rim of Canyon Country Club's famous golf course, differs in that here one developer wanted to copy another developer's house. New York–based developer Robert Grundt and his wife liked the Alexander Residence so much that they asked Krisel to do a version for them. And while it's true that the plans of the houses are similar, the Tipper-Grundt Residence occupies a very different site with a different ambiance . . . which in turn generated a different, and *custom,* response. You'd have to know both houses fairly well to suspect a relationship.

Beginning with the Alexander Residence, it's not surprising that it is the most adventurous and high-spirited of the three. That's as it should be: it illustrates the same spirit that led Bob Alexander and his father, George, to help define the area's unique identity within Midcentury Modernism, an identity populated by some 1,200 Modern tract houses of theirs. Helene Alexander was smitten with her surprise; right under her nose, Bob had conveniently built it in full view as the "House of Tomorrow," ostensibly to market the firm's commitment to the future. With a knowing smile, Bill Krisel recalled that Helene immediately wanted to move out of the "crappy" tract home the Alexanders lived in (which of course Krisel also designed).

Much of the dwelling's fame, however, isn't because of the Alexanders (who died in a plane accident in 1965). Rather, the home's renown rests on its brief tenure as Elvis and Priscilla Presley's honeymoon hideaway. The audaciousness of moves such as a sixty-four-foot-long curved sofa certainly fit the reputation of the bigger-than-life "King." However, there is another, slightly delicious move that speaks to Eros. The house is sited on the rising slope of Vista Las Palmas (the neighborhood, not the tract of the same name.) As you approach the house from below, an angled volume of wood and glass juts out well above a

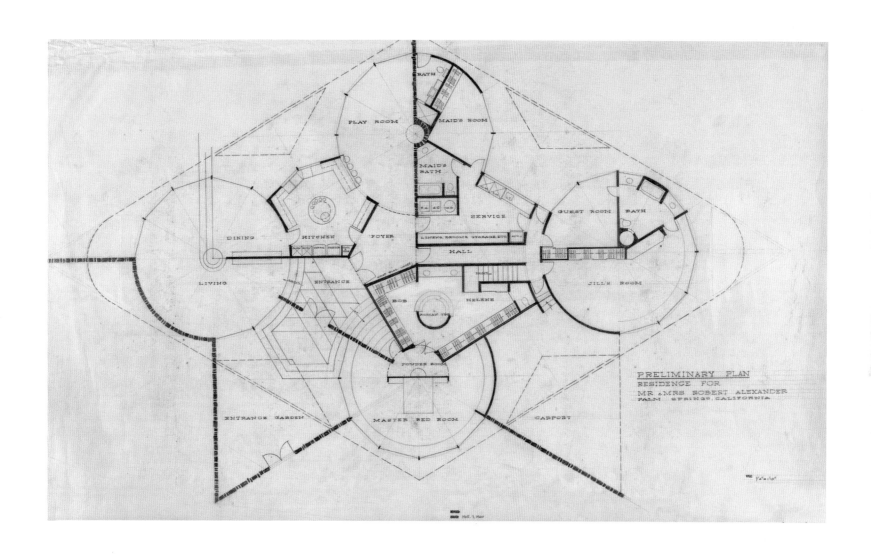

Preliminary plan for the House of Tomorrow,
Palm Springs, California, showing pods
(March 7, 1960)—detail.

RESIDENCE for MR. & MRS. ROBERT ALEXANDER   PALM SPRINGS

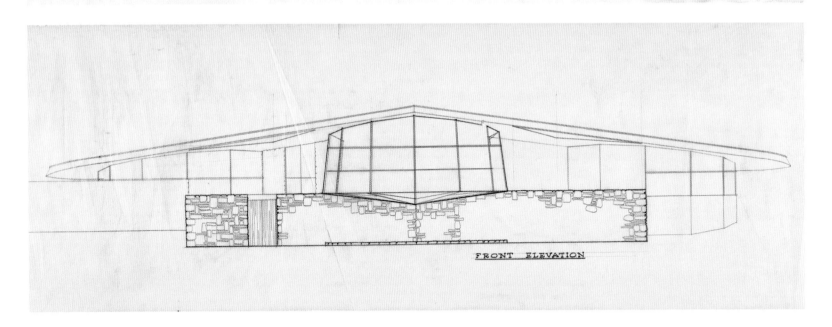

FRONT ELEVATION

Above: Rendering of preliminary design for the House of Tomorrow, Vista Las Palmas, Palm Springs, California (1959).

Below: Drawing of the front elevation for the House of Tomorrow, as built, Vista Las Palmas, Palm Springs, California (circa 1960).

Facing: Robert Doisneau (1912–94), on assignment for *Fortune* magazine, photographs a model of the Alexander Residence, known as the House of Tomorrow, with the house under construction in the background (November 1960). This image is usually published incorrectly in reverse. While Doisneau is identified as the photographer, the person who took the photograph of Doisneau is not the architect, William Krisel, as some had thought.

KRISEL GOES CUSTOM **143**

Helene and Bob Alexander enjoying their new living room in the House of Tomorrow, Vista Las Palmas, Palm Springs, California (1962). Note the wok-like fireplace that cantilevers over the terrazzo steps leading up to the dining area.

Cal Bernstein, photographer, Look Magazine Photograph Collection, Library of Congress, Prints & Photographs Division (reproduction number LC-L9-63-9882, color slide #29).

recessed stone wall and the offset landscaped entrance that layers stepping stones, short bridges, landings, and waterfalls. That jutting volume, part of one of a quartet of octagons, contains the master bedroom suite. The elevated height preserves privacy while adding a frisson of excitement to the possibilities. Without that height, putting the master bedroom above the entrance would be decidedly subversive.[2] But locating the master octagon on the east, Krisel also ensured lovely morning light as well as a commanding view of the Coachella Valley and the hilly Little San Bernardino and Santa Rosa ranges to the east and south. In the '60s at night, the view must have captured coming rain and windstorms and the scattered light of a much more modest Palm Springs amidst the dark, velvety landscape of distant mountains below a sky of stars. Bob Alexander could survey the progress of his developments spread out before him, a rather different kingdom than Presley ever enjoyed.

The singer's celebrity notwithstanding, what is really interesting here is how Krisel synthesized what he knew—and loved—about the Alexander family, and how he integrated that knowledge into the site. Krisel's parti pris (overall concept) began with what is called a "bubble diagram." For any architect, such a diagram is a standard tool that groups functions according to a particular spatial area. In the Alexanders' case it divided the area into four zones: one for the master bedroom; the second for living and eating; the third as guest suite and bedroom for the Alexanders' young daughter, Jill; and the fourth for play and servants' quarters. The "bubbles" were then almost literally translated into circles and curves, elements always present in some form in Krisel's work. So far, pretty standard. But an outstanding piece of architecture often starts with a standard technique . . . and then transcends it.

As the idea for the four large "pods" emerged, so did the consideration of the rocky sloping site. Given Krisel's experience with desert topography, he knew better than to excavate. Instead, he *added* material to fill in the spaces between the boulders, just as the spaces between each circle became opportunities for interstitial spaces themselves—corridors, staircases, the kitchen, and an imposing entrance foyer. Each octagon-circle is on a different elevation, yet all are sheltered by a single sloping roof.

The exterior wood-and-stucco frames became octagons to accommodate the realities of construction and materials (especially glass). By contrast, other elements, such as the sofa, assumed the task of maintaining the circle as a primary motif. Its shamelessly long curve defines the circumference of the circle tangent to and within the octagon. Both the round, freestanding kitchen range island and fireplace are essentially plays on circles of various diameters. Outside, Krisel chose circles for the calibrated sequence of stepping stones leading to the front door across short waterfalls and pools. "Circles have no leading edge," Krisel says. "You can approach them from anywhere."[3] That architectural gentleness, verbally conveyed as "no leading edge," accommodates an approach from a variety of points. In contrast, the roof doesn't interact directly with the body. Thus it is free to introduce sharp angles into the equation. The angles add aesthetic exhilaration while sheltering the windows, and its seemingly oddly shaped cutouts introduce dynamic ways to experience daylight on the interior. The roundedness at the ground plane and the angles above are equally user-friendly. Just in different ways.

As one proceeds through the house, it's clear that locating the master bedroom above the entrance was smart in another way. After entering the foyer, Krisel cleverly oriented the visitors away from the bedroom and towards the living room. Originally, a pony wall (a wall that is not full height) extended a little ways into the circle, distinguishing the living and dining areas. Beyond, the sustained curve of the

The House of Tomorrow (2015).
Note how the roof appears to float
above the two visible room pods.

Photograph © Darren Bradley.

sofa beckoned the visitor to walk around the wall to discover what had been hidden from view—the pool, surrounded by lush landscaping and extended terraces. Of the many changes to the house, Krisel mourns the demolition of the pony wall by a later owner, because of the critical role it played in creating mystery—that sense of anticipation delayed and then resolved.[4] Like a conductor, the wall also directed the sense of flowing space so profoundly witnessed here. The term, now so overused as to be mind-numbingly predictable in all manner of academic and shelter magazines, really meant something here. Anchored by that pony wall, space flowed here, forming whirlpools and then spilling over broad interior steps and low furniture that feels set into the earth. Without the wall, space runs wild, ricocheting all over incoherently, and the visitor has lost the opportunity to experience that sensation of mystery.

As a relaxed, elongated grouping of long horizontals and rectilinear volumes that seem to skim the earth like a white glider, the Kemp Residence is a different creature altogether. Occupying flat land on a curving corner suburban site, the U-shaped house embodies a very fine attention to choreographing the transition from street to house. Behind a later masonry wall built to secure privacy, the house is set amidst a luxuriant landscape of desert natives, cacti, yucca, dignified groupings of desert fan palms (complete with lavish skirts, signaling history and longevity), green lawns, and dark, leafy plantings set into rounded beds of decomposed granite or pebbles.

The entrance is conceived as a formal series of detached and semidetached U-shaped frames, emphasizing the sense of procession to the deeply recessed front door. The first frame is a freestanding stucco "collar" connected to a light wooden frame, which in turn meets a tall wall of slump stone masonry. Perpendicular to the frames, the wall shields the long entrance from view. Thus the multivalent passage

Jill Alexander (left) with staffers Will and Thelma in the House of Tomorrow kitchen (1962). Note the hourglass-shaped vent similar to the living room fireplace, and stove burners built directly into the circular countertop below the domed indoor barbecue.

Cal Bernstein, photographer, Look Magazine Photograph Collection Library of Congress, Prints & Photographs Division (reproduction number LC-L9-63-9882, color slide #11).

The Alexanders and friends party like it's 1962. Note the cutout in the roof canopy that allowed light into the patio.

Cal Bernstein, photographer, Look Magazine Photograph Collection, Library of Congress, Prints & Photographs Division (reproduction number LC-L9-63-9882, color slide #36).

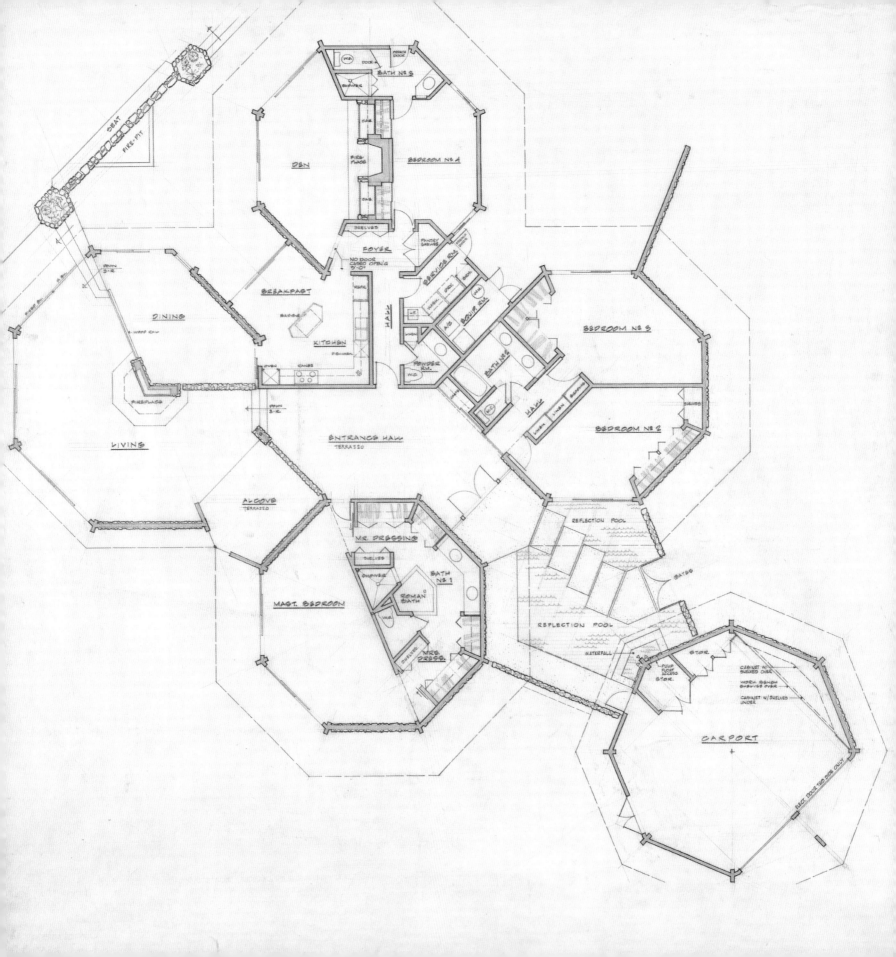

Facing: The second version of the plan for what would eventually be known as the Tipper-Grundt Residence (1968)—detail.

Below: Rendering of the Robert Grundt Residence, viewed from the fairway of the Canyon Country Club (1967)—detail. Note the interior is carefully detailed, with fireplace, books, and chairs clearly visible.

OWNER: MR. & MRS. ROBERT GRUNDT

WILLIAM KRISEL A.I.A.

architecture · planning · landscaping
12205 Santa Monica Boulevard / Los Angeles 25, California
478-0955

110 West C Street   Suite 812
San Diego 1, California, 232-3255

REV. | DATE: | REV. | DATE:

from street to entrance is rather ennobling in mediating and slowing the procession before entering the cool interior. From above, the various shading devices mean that the sun strikes a visitor's shoulders in a gradation from full sunlight to dappled light to welcoming shadow by the time one presses the buzzer.

The idea for replacing standard concrete block with slump stone, with its varied, textured surface, was perhaps Kemp's single contribution to the design. If so, it was a masterstroke that Krisel embraced. The stone face invites a dynamic play of light and shadow . . . and as Albert Frey once told the author, "architecture is all about light and shadow, isn't that why we are in Palm Springs?"

In the Kemp plan, the large, graceful U-shaped building surrounds a long, rectangular pool. The open area at the south is devoted to lounging, barbecuing, and relaxing. Broad terraces around the pool lead to rooms with full-height glass walls.

Each bedroom had its own private low-walled patio that opened to the landscape on the outside of the "U"; those walls have disappeared. Krisel also included individual terraces for the kitchen and the family room, creating outdoor spaces tailored to utility or casual family time. Overall, the different character of each of these outdoor "rooms" not only enlarged interior space, but provided yet more ways to use and experience space; that is a rather theoretical concept, perhaps, but not in practice, because we humans quickly learn how to exploit such latent opportunities.

Krisel also designed an open-air atrium at the southwest end of the house. It was later demolished and enclosed to accommodate an enlarged master bathroom. Terminating a long east–west passageway, the atrium's task was to draw the visitor down the corridor, anticipating the promise of light and greenery. Open to the sky, a sliding glass wall in the original master bathroom opened into the atrium. This strategy distinguished the master suite from the other bedrooms in two ways. While each of the other bedrooms enjoyed a private outdoor terrace, the inhabitants of the master suite were privileged to an experience of nature that was both more sensual and more sheltered, especially from wind and sun. The loss of this intimate experience is a casualty that the architect is quick to point out. Even with these alterations, however, the "Lost Krisel" has lost none of its Shangri-la magic. It is very much a midcentury oasis in the desert.

The last of the three houses, the Tipper-Grundt Residence, is the story of how determination and a well-endowed wallet can win the prize.[5]

The Grundts acquired a flat site facing the fairway of the famous Canyon Country Club golf course. The parcel terminates a secluded cul-de-sac. Here, Krisel used the four-octagon idea that he employed for the Alexanders, and added a fifth for the garage. However, rather than a single and sharply angled roof sheltering all the spaces, here each octagon has its own roof, which boasts a rather unusual feature. To hide mechanical equipment, a central spire rises from each "pod," as though the roof had been pulled up like fabric from a middle point. Thus, from a distance the decentralized, rather reserved house looks more like a grouping of dwellings rather than one residence.

During construction, the site had a frequent visitor. A man began stopping at the job site every day, asking questions and studying Krisel plans that were kept on the site. Eventually he approached the Grundts and asked to buy the house. He was flatly refused; after all, Krisel had designed this dream house for them. After sustained talks, the Grundts agreed to a sale. The man insisted on three changes, none

Early concept drawing for the living room of the Robert Grundt Residence, with a fireplace rising up through the central spire of the pod (circa 1967).

of them to the house but instead, surprisingly, to the garage: the walls were to be lined with niches and shelving; its floor was to be terrazzo rather than standard concrete; and the space was to be air-conditioned. Krisel met the man once and easily implemented the changes.

The stranger turned out to be Maynard Tipper, who invented the "Tipper Casing Tyer" in 1952, revolutionizing the sausage casings industry with a clip-and-tying machine that replaced hand labor.[6] Tipper must have been a shrewd businessman as well as an inventor, because throughout the 1950s and '60s he obtained over a dozen patents connected to the tying method and apparatus. The inventions made him a very wealthy man, who nonetheless wanted to continue experimenting in his now rather remarkable garage: a terrazzo floor, after all, is not only far more handsome but more impervious to fluids—a quality of no little importance to a man whose inventions may have had more influence in American food culture than we realize.

Left: Tipper-Grundt Residence,
Palm Springs, California (2011).
Note the Polynesian elements,
such as the outriggers extending
from the roof and rock walls.

Photograph by John Crosse,
from his collection.

Overleaf: Rendering of
the Kemp Residence
(1963)—detail.

Gift of William and Corinne Krisel.
William Krisel Architectural Archive,
Getty Research Institute, Los Angeles
(2009.M.23). © J. Paul Getty Trust.

Backyard view of the Lost Krisel,
Palm Desert, California, as it looks today
(2013).

Photograph by James Schnepf/
Palm Springs Modern Living.

The Lost Krisel as it looks today.

Kemp Residence, Palm Desert, California

(2013).

Photograph by James Schnepf/
Palm Springs Modern Living.

NOTES

1. Such a clerestory followed the line of a sloped roof at the top of the glazing, while the bottom of the window was held to a straight line. The feature can be seen in many residential works by postwar architects, who were often graduates of USC, including Buff, Straub and Hensman; Randell Makinson; A. Quincy Jones, and Frederick Emmons (with whom Jones designed tract homes for developer Joseph Eichler). The angled clerestory, a great device for preserving privacy while illuminating the interior, was typically one element in a larger post-and-beam construction. While a popular motif that unified a special period of significance for postwar residential architecture in California it should be noted that each architect, including Krisel, interpreted the detail differently.

2. In the interest of the history of Modernism in Southern California, there is an early example of the unusual positioning of bedrooms, or sleeping quarters, directly above the front entrance. Rudolph Schindler's iconic King's Road House in Los Angeles (1922), features "sleeping baskets" suspended from a frame directly above the recessed front door. Both Schindler's and Krisel's bold relocation of a function usually set well into a home exemplifies a belief that ignores conventional thinking about spatial proprieties.

3. William Krisel, interview with Barbara Lamprecht, July 22, 2015.

4. The idea of mystery is employed in the discipline of environmental psychology, which has long investigated the physiological and psychological factors in human interactions with their environments. How much complexity, engagement, understanding, mystery, and involvement is desirable in an environment varies according to who is involved and what their activities are. An extended full-height wall that may harbor a predator and engender primal fear is one thing; a pony wall that can be quickly navigated to reveal a delightful surprise is quite another. The height and length of Krisel's pony wall at the Alexander Residence demonstrates he understood this intuitively.

5. Although not explored here, the underlying story is the role of Jews in Palm Springs. Like the Tamarisk Country Club, the Canyon Country Club and golf course were established in 1962 by Jewish retailers, entertainers, and other professionals. They leased tribal land from the Agua Caliente Band of Cahuilla Indians, a tale of diversity Palm Springs style. Architectural historian Peter Moruzzi discusses the influence of Jewish life in Palm Springs in *Palm Springs Holiday* (Layton, Utah: Gibbs Smith, 2009).

6. The Tipper Tie Group, part of the Dover Corporation, has offices in Germany, Switzerland, and North Carolina. It celebrated its golden anniversary in 2002.

8 landscape architecture

J. C. MILLER

"[Drawing] is the way I express my Modern design language. I like to solve problems quickly [through drawing] and without too many words."

— WILLIAM KRISEL

When entering one of the many desert homes designed by William Krisel, with its soaring asymmetrical roofline gesturing to nearby mountains, walls of glass that open rooms to expansive vistas, and dynamic blending of spaces both inside and out, it is not always clear where architecture ends and landscape architecture might begin. Krisel is unapologetic about any confusion: "I don't think of landscape architecture as a separate activity. I would no more ignore that aspect of the design or pass it to someone else than I would leave out the climate control or plumbing."[1]

Underlying this seemingly effortless combination is a consciously applied design vocabulary, a language that addresses landscape with the same care and respect as structure. The resulting environments are extraordinary and enduring examples of the best Midcentury Modern design, blending site and structure in a way that is timeless and instantly recognizable. It is difficult to find parallels even among the most recognizable masterpieces of Midcentury Modernism.

Facing: Backyard view of a tract home built, landscaped, and furnished by Krisel for the Alexander family, with Corinne Krisel as the model (1957).

Photograph by Julius Shulman.
Getty Research Institute, Los Angeles
(2004.R.10). © J. Paul Getty Trust.

Above: This detail from an elevation drawing depicting the screen block walls and planting proposed for the Canyon View Estates development in Palm Springs is typical of the artistic representations that Krisel provided to his clients. In this drawing the proposed plants, concrete screen wall, and even the character of the landscape boulders are rendered in great detail.

Gift of William and Corinne Krisel. William Krisel Architectural Archive, Getty Research Institute, Los Angeles (2009.M.23). © J. Paul Getty Trust.

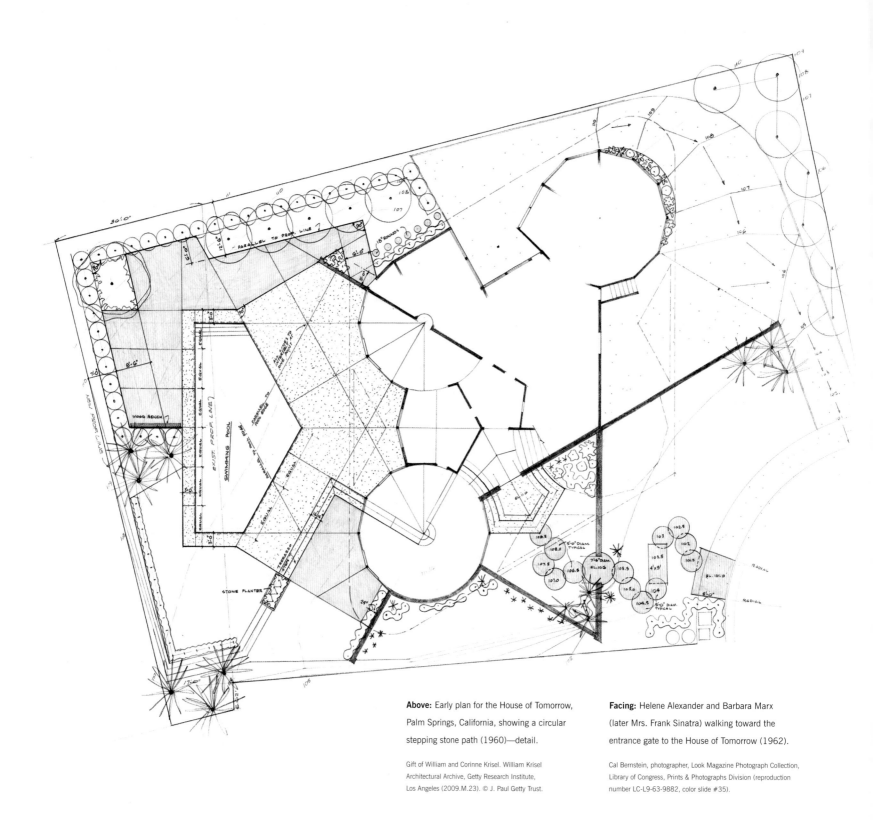

Above: Early plan for the House of Tomorrow, Palm Springs, California, showing a circular stepping stone path (1960)—detail.

Facing: Helene Alexander and Barbara Marx (later Mrs. Frank Sinatra) walking toward the entrance gate to the House of Tomorrow (1962).

EARLY INFLUENCES

Krisel became interested in landscape architecture and its potential as a medium for modern design while a student at the University of Southern California. Upon his return to school after service in World War II, Krisel enrolled in a two-semester course taught by prominent midcentury landscape architect Garrett Eckbo.[2]

This class made him aware of the potential to employ a Modernist design vocabulary beyond the building envelope. Eckbo encouraged his students to engage outdoor spaces as functional equivalents to rooms and Krisel took this fundamental aspect of landscape to heart. When recalling this period at USC, he remembers Eckbo holding his hand up during a lecture and looking at the class through his spread fingers, talking about how to use plant material and landscape elements to manage views, add interest, and define spaces. Krisel adopted this approach and worked with the landscape as a means of extending the design function across the site. His goal was to create uninhibited flow between exterior and interior spaces. After graduation he maintained an ongoing professional relationship with Eckbo and invited him to participate on the Ocotillo Lodge project in Palm Springs. Landscape design was more than a peripheral interest for Krisel, and in 1954 he obtained his landscape architecture license, an unusual move for an architect.

THE INFLUENCE OF ART AND THE IMPORTANCE OF PERSPECTIVE DRAWING ON LANDSCAPE DESIGN

Krisel acknowledges that his designed spaces have a strong graphic quality, especially recent work in Palm Springs. He understands why some might try to make a connection between strongly expressed forms and modern art, but he is quick to point out that his work, while artful, is a design response to client need and the functional requirements of the site. His built work is the manifestation of a guiding design language, not art made for the sake of art.

Certainly he refined the composition of exterior design elements for visual appeal, but unlike a painter working in a Modernist style, he is not trying to evoke a response by using landscape materials in a purely abstract manner. In this he differs from other postwar landscape architects, including his early mentor Eckbo, whose work made direct reference to early-twentieth-century abstract painters.[3]

While the creation of fine art may not have been his primary goal, the sketches, plans, and elevations that he produced throughout his career certainly show him in the artist's role. Filled with expressive human figures and richly detailed and precise depictions of plants, Krisel's drawings worked as both a design technique and a promotional device, as they were often used by builder clients in sales brochures. Krisel devoted considerable time to perspective drawing throughout the design process. Because such works are difficult to produce, they are often limited to speculative drawings of conceptual ideas, or made after the fact to document a final design. Krisel's skill in perspective drawing allowed him this luxury throughout the design process. When discussing his method, he explained that he always began with a drawing that explored building layout and site design in a combined plan. When the floor plans and landscape shapes and forms had developed to a certain point, he would move into three-dimensional perspective drawing to verify the compositional relationships between built structures and site features, including irregular elements such as trees.[4]

Gardens in the Twin Palms neighborhood in Palm Springs provided the opportunity for Krisel to apply his Modern design language from curb to back fence line. In this view of a classic design, the bold shapes of crisply defined gravel beds are as important to the composition as the roofline (circa 1957).

The Menrad Residence,
Twin Palms, Palm Springs,
California, with its geometric
landscaping (2015).

Photograph © Darren Bradley.

Top: Exterior view of a house in Twin Palms, Palm Springs, California (2015). Note the landscape patterns done with colored stone that reflects the architecture of the house and draws it out into the landscape.

Photograph © Darren Bradley.

Bottom: Exterior view of a house in Twin Palms, Palm Springs, California (2015). Note the large curving landscape that draws the eye around to the side of the home, especially visible on this corner lot. Patterns are created using special rubber mulch in various colors.

Photograph © Darren Bradley.

when our office was very busy I did all the landscape plans—no one else understood how to do that work, what the symbols meant or how to set out plants for effect."[5] Krisel underscores the important and efficient role of drawing in his design process when he says, "It [drawing] is the way I express my Modern design language. I like to solve problems quickly [through drawing] and without too many words."[6]

DEVELOPING A MODERN LANGUAGE FOR LANDSCAPE

As he created site designs for larger and more complex projects, Krisel's language for landscape evolved. Spaces associated with the building that allowed direct access in and out of the structure and blurred the lines between interior and exterior can be found in his earliest residential designs. Such spaces are fundamental to a Modernist emphasis on function and spatial definition, and as a result are often extensively paved and defined by landscape walls, screens, arbors, or other structures. Taking advantage of California's climate, he often included small entry courtyards, planted patios outside of bedrooms, and larger terraces, often with small trees, adjacent to the public rooms of his residential designs. These indoor/outdoor spaces were scaled to the domestic environment and afforded comfortable spaces for small groups. In his larger-scale desert work, we see the remarkable evolution of these residential spaces into outdoor great rooms sized to accommodate larger numbers of people and a variety of activities. The swimming pool was the central feature of these spaces and in many ways the heart of the development.

His work on Ocotillo Lodge, his earliest desert project for the Alexander Construction Company, created the opportunity for research into the building types and landscape

His ability to make complex and accurate perspective drawings was an especially important tool for communicating design ideas. The large-scale relationships between structures and their surroundings were convincing and authoritative because of the accuracy he was able to achieve. When viewed in a contemporary context of similar drawings produced by means of computer modeling, his hand drafting and rendering skills are all the more remarkable.

Enjoyable in retrospect as art, the drawings produced by Krisel were also an integral part of the design process. Drawing, both illustrative and technical, was of particular importance to his practice as a landscape architect. "Even

Rendering of the Bob and Helene Alexander Residence
in Twin Palms, featuring furniture and landscape layout,
Palm Springs, California (circa 1957)—detail.

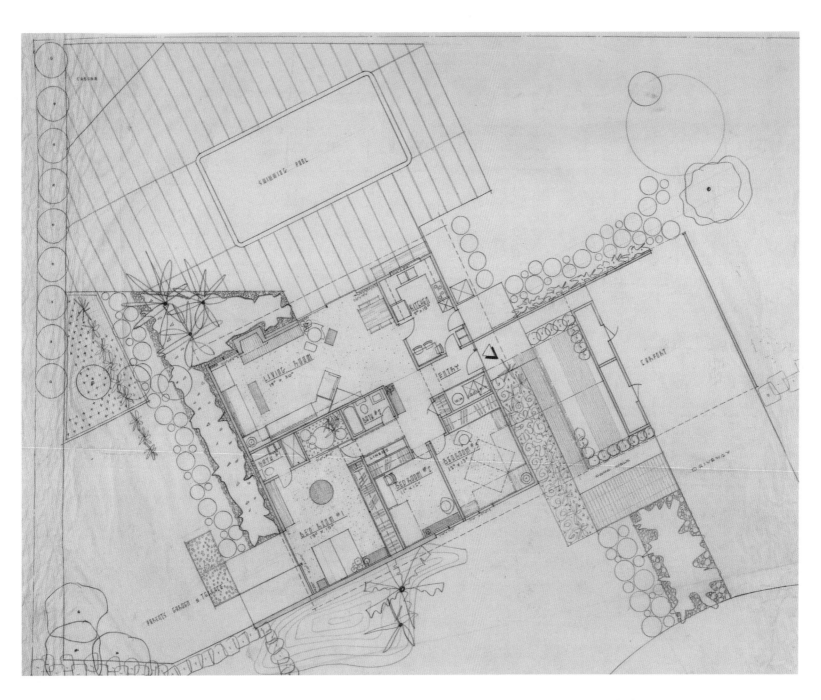

a landscape design is to remain legible over time in that sometimes harsh environment.

Responding to this need, the network of pathways found in his desert work are typically made of poured-in-place concrete, sometimes colored or textured to coordinate with the materials of nearby architecture. Site walls were more often than not made of concrete shadow blocks, a staple material of Midcentury Modern architecture that he helped invent and popularize. In a landscape plan prepared by William Krisel, pathways and site walls do not wander in naturalistic curves; rather they strike bold lines, reinforcing geometries that he repeats in the architecture. In some cases stepping-stone-type paths are provided in lieu of a full paving where he hoped to establish a hierarchy. While these less-formal tracks might meander slightly in a pleasingly irregular way, there is still a crisp geometry to be found in the perfect concrete circles that define each step.

Shade was an integral part of the comprehensive environments that Krisel designed. An obvious response to human need in the desert environment, Krisel animated the snack bars, equipment and changing rooms, ramadas, and arbors found on his pool decks with the same liveliness and precise geometry as his buildings. With these simple open structures he achieved dramatic design lines, defined edges, and created overhead planes. The curved arbor at Ocotillo Lodge included a built-in bench, and perimeter planting established an edge that framed views of the pool, not unlike the large walls of glass that separated the restaurant dining room from the pool deck.

The swimming pool holds a central position, quite literally, in the postwar California landscape. Thomas Church, arguably the leading landscape architect of the period, devoted an entire section—no less than twenty pages—to this garden feature in his classic book *Gardens Are for People.*

Bright orange paint is used on both the vertical supports for the shade trellis and the clubhouse canopy at Ocotillo Lodge. Orange flowering bougainvillea was planted behind the arbor to further the coordinated color scheme (circa 1957).

Photograph by Garrett Eckbo. Courtesy of Marc Treib.

features important to desert leisure. For that project a central space appropriate as the primary outdoor social gathering spot for a resort hotel was developed. The space included a large swimming pool, ample paved areas for lounge chairs and tables, concrete walkways, and an edge-defining shade arbor that completed the circular form of the building. A snack bar with patio seating was located behind the arbor, slightly apart from the center of the space. Krisel's later designs for multiple-unit residential projects in the desert included many of the features and landscape elements first explored for Ocotillo Lodge.

Walls, paved pathways, structures such as arbors, screens, or ramadas, and swimming pools are built elements in the landscape that are often referred to as "hardscape." These landscape features formed an important vocabulary for Krisel as he worked in the intense climate of the Coachella Valley. Durability and longevity are absolute requirements if

Church explained to homeowners and other designers the wide range of design possibilities for the pool in terms of both function and form, and introduced the world to the idea of the kidney-shaped pool.[7] Despite Church's advice as to the myriad design possibilities, the majority of midcentury pools ended up dominating the garden and restricting other activities, since they were placed in the middle of the garden. Certainly this was due in part to the fact that for the average residential lot it was the largest single feature in a garden of limited size.

While still centrally located and prominent, the swimming pool took on a different character when addressed by Krisel. He saw the pool as a space-organizing device and an opportunity to expand and apply the same design vocabulary used in the buildings and across the site. The shape of the pool at Ocotillo Lodge is an early example of this. Avoiding the temptation to simply reinforce the curved building wall with a circular pool, the form is drawn in at angles to create an asymmetrical hourglass-like form with rounded ends. The dynamic geometry of the pool deck adds interest to the view of the pool from the dining room and also serves to increase the available space for outdoor furniture, an important consideration at a busy hotel. It also reduces the size of the pool, and therefore the expense of constructing and maintaining it. Subsequent site designs for desert condominium developments offered the opportunity to refine this pool design strategy. In those situations the shape of the pool is subtly influenced by site topography. This is especially noticeable when comparing the swimming pools designed for the various phases of the Sandpiper development in Palm Desert, where the pools echo the geometries of the broad terraced retaining walls.

Krisel's language of design is not limited to hardscape features; it also includes planting. His ideas on plant selection

Astute plant selection is a key concern for longevity of design, especially in a desert climate. Krisel selected plants with high heat tolerance for the pool deck at Sandpiper 1. Beyond their function as durable markers in the landscape, the distinctive vertical character of the planting provides an attractive foil to the strong lines of the architecture and ground plane (circa 1958).

Krisel's innovative stepped retaining walls—he calls them horizontal walls— were a visually dramatic and cost-effective design response to the sloped site. The Sandpiper received considerable professional acclaim, garnering awards for architectural and landscape design shortly after construction of the first phase was complete. It is still regarded as Krisel's landscape masterpiece (circa 1958).

Photograph by Julius Shulman.
Getty Research Institute,
Los Angeles (2004.R.10).
© J. Paul Getty Trust.

originate in concepts learned at USC, where Garrett Eckbo's teaching focused on the use of plants as design elements. This innovative approach to planting advocated for function, arrangement, and maintenance over the traditionally taught pictorial and sentimental strategies.[8] His teaching did not address in detail the specific needs of plant species or horticultural knowledge. Krisel recalls that Eckbo handed out information on plants and plant lists that described form, size, color, and texture. From this early information, Krisel developed his own plant palette that focused plant choices primarily on design function. At the conceptual stage of building and site design, he would lay out planting areas to address grading concerns and provide boundary or transition spaces, and then select appropriate plant species to achieve a desired effect, such as a vertical focal point or visual screening. As work progressed he would vet his plant choices with locally knowledgeable plant specialists, often experienced landscape contractors, and refine his initial planting decisions.[9]

Krisel made a habit of revisiting his built projects whenever possible to observe plant growth, and based on these observations refined his understanding of the plants that could be depended on to achieve his goals in the challenging climate of the Coachella Valley. He notes that, "Of course people make changes and over time it can look quite different from the original, but you can still tell what [planting] has done well and what has fared poorly or disappeared."[10] A basic tenet of Modern design is that it should demonstratively improve the daily experience of those who live in and around it.[11] Krisel's thoughtful planting design does just that—maximizing enjoyment while minimizing the cost and effort of maintenance. This is design thinking especially appropriate in the desert communities, where the environments he created were often getaways where relief was sought from the rigors of mowing the lawn or clipping hedges.

DESIGN PROCESS AND METHODOLOGY

To fully appreciate the complete nature of a Krisel-designed environment it is worthwhile to look briefly at the structure of his professional design practice and his integrated design process. His office was unique in that it offered nearly all of the skills in-house necessary to support a development project. In addition to the typical services offered by his peers such as site planning, building design, and construction cost estimating, Krisel provided interior design, graphic design, and site design, including lighting and landscape architecture. Since he envisioned, managed, and in most cases directly produced each of these different aspects of the project, he was able to achieve a level of coherence in his designed environments that would have been difficult, if not impossible, for a team of separate professionals. Although the pressure imposed by that centralized responsibility must have at times been difficult to bear, the resultant organizational structure allowed his design voice—in Krisel's words, the language of Modernism—to be clearly heard.

While the language of William Krisel achieves lyrical results, it is not the language of poetry; rather it is a discourse rooted in analytical process and problem solving. Every commission began with research. Initial meetings with new clients focused on the development of a program to which the design would respond. The needs and priorities of the client were articulated and budgets were established. If the project type was something new to him, Krisel would do further background research—for example, studying the specific operations of the hospitality industry to better design a hotel property early in his career. This guided his thinking for the duration of the project. Armed with an understanding of what was needed, Krisel examined the physical aspects of the site, including topography, views, and prevailing winds, as well as invisible constraints such as building codes and utility services. The purpose of site analysis was to determine what characteristics of the site could be developed and improved in service to the design program.

With the research complete, Krisel could begin the complex process of integrated design. An important aspect of this process was the method that he used to generate plans for design and construction. Work began with a base sheet that included the proposed building locations, property lines, and topography. Floor plans, developed in tandem with landscape features, were started. To this drawing he would add detailed line work, often color coded, for each of the various aspects of the landscape: paving and walkway layout, grading, irrigation, planting, lighting, etc. Adjustments and refinements were made to all aspects of the design as he made repeated passes over the plan while developing a master drawing. Specific subdrawings such as planting or irrigation plans were created for use by construction contractors only after he had developed a satisfactory comprehensive plan.[12] This method differed from the (still) standard practice in which each design discipline worked independently on their respective parts of the design and then compared and coordinated drawings after the fact. Because of this unique production strategy, Krisel was able to identify potential conflict between disparate systems in real time as the drawing developed, and as a result, construction of his projects was efficient and costs were kept low.

When William Krisel talks about design it does not take long for the conversation to turn to problem solving. As a result of his education and early career association with Garrett Eckbo, he was well versed in the conceptual framework that guided modern landscape architecture in the postwar period. This awareness coupled with a strong creative vision informed his early design strategies, but abstraction was always tempered by functional pragmatism.

Krisel's language is above all pragmatic. This quality is especially apparent in the development projects for large-scale residential builders. Easy replication and budget-minded solutions critical for the success of this work provided Krisel ample opportunity to develop and refine his landscape vocabulary. While some prominent designers of the midcentury period eschewed it because of the perceived constraints, Krisel embraced the challenges of market-driven design with characteristic confidence and enthusiasm. Reflecting on his work with large-scale builders such as the Alexander Construction Company, he notes that while somewhat different, the goals of the designer and the developer are not inconsistent. "For the builder client the bottom line was a profitable development; for me it was good design, and this worked out. Buyers were attracted to the homes and they sold well."[13]

Large-scale tract work in Palm Springs and neighboring desert communities offered him the opportunity to apply

Facing: Sandpiper Circle 2 landscape plan,
Palm Desert, California (1959)—detail.

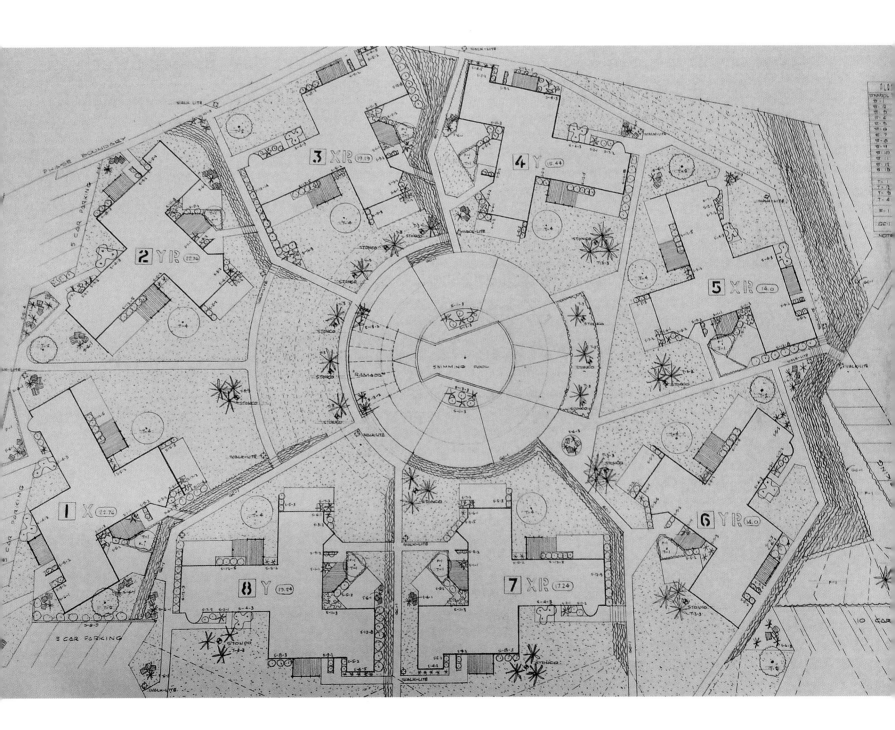

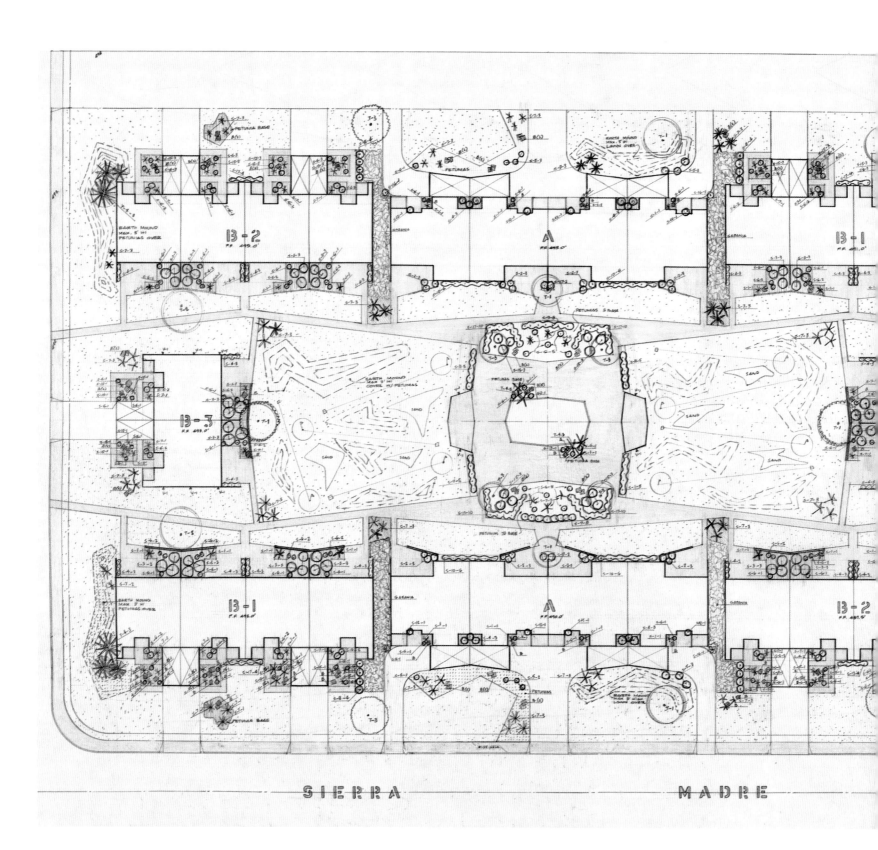

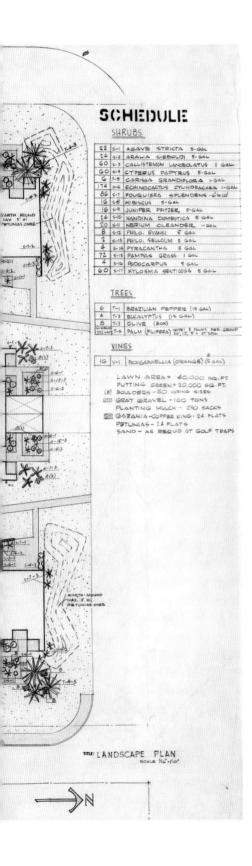

SCHEDULE

SHRUBS

22	S-1	AGAVE STRICTA	5-GAL
24	S-2	ARALIA SIEBOLDI	5-GAL
60	S-3	CALLISTEMON LANCEOLATUS	1 GAL
60	S-4	CYPERUS PAPYRUS	5-GAL
6	S-5	CARISSA GRANDIFLORA	1-GAL
174	S-6	ECHINOCACTUS CYLINDRACEA	1-GAL
86	S-7	FOUQUIERA SPLENDENS	6' to 10'
16	S-8	HIBISCUS	5-GAL
16	S-9	JUNIPER PFITZER	5-GAL
24	S-10	NANDINA DOMESTICA	5 GAL
20	S-11	NERIUM OLEANDER	1-GAL
8	S-12	PHILO. EVANSI	5 GAL
2	S-13	PHILO. SELLOUM	5 GAL
4	S-14	PYRACANTHA	5 GAL
72	S-15	PAMPAS GRASS	1 GAL
4	S-16	PODOCARPUS	5 GAL
60	S-17	XYLOSMA SENTICOSA	5 GAL

TREES

6	T-1	BRAZILIAN PEPPER	(15 GAL)
4	T-2	EUCALYPTUS	(15 GAL)
8	T-3	OLIVE	(BOX)
	T-4	PALM (FILIFERA)	

VINES

16	V-1	BOUGAINVILLEA (ORANGE)	(5 GAL)

LAWN AREA = 40,000 SQ.FT.
PUTTING GREEN = 20,000 SQ.FT.
BOULDERS - 50 VARING SITES
GRAY GRAVEL - 100 TONS
PLANTING MULCH - 250 SACKS
GAZANIA-COPPER KING - 24 FLATS
PETUNIAS - 24 FLATS
SAND - AS REQUID AT GOLF TRAPS

TITLE: LANDSCAPE PLAN

N

Modernist principles at a neighborhood scale. Even as they were being built in unfathomable numbers, the typical postwar American residential suburb was criticized as bland, stifling, and monotonous. As he was grappling with the design challenges of large tract development, Krisel utilized a number of landscape strategies to add vitality and individuality to his projects.

A relentless pursuit of variety in all aspects of design differentiates Krisel's language when applied at a neighborhood scale. He understood that repetition gave rise to the anonymous and depressing quality of many postwar suburbs. Rather than simply placing the building in the same position on the lot relative to the property lines and setbacks, he adjusted the locations to the greatest degree possible. The site plan and building placements he developed at the Sandpiper condominiums are a strong example of this. For that project he varied the location and orientation of each home to maximize solar benefits and shade cast by the building, an especially welcome feature for homes in that hot climate. The Sandpiper, a complex project built in multiple phases in Palm Desert, along with Ocotillo Lodge and adjacent Twin Palms neighborhood in Palm Springs, offer an opportunity to look closely at his language of design at a variety of scales.

Landscaping plan, Canyon View Estates,
Palm Springs, California (undated)—detail.

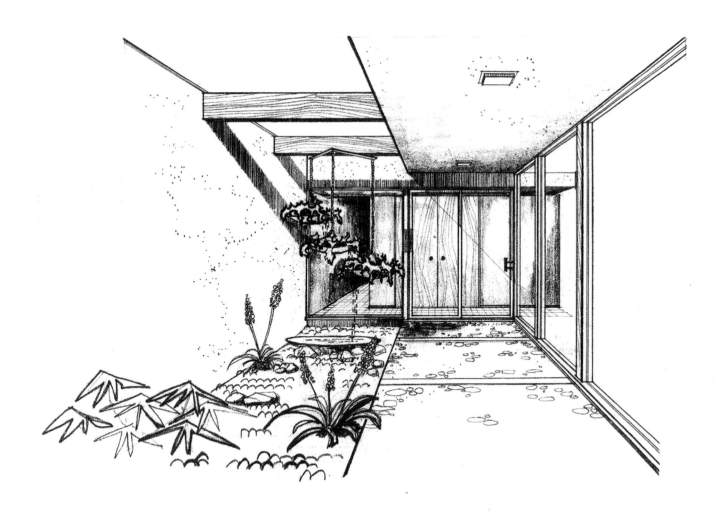

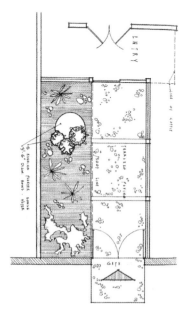

Facing: Detail of trellis shading in
a home entranceway, Twin Palms,
Palm Springs, California (2015).

Photograph © Darren Bradley.

Above and left: Semi-enclosed entry patios provided a transition between the public and private realms in many units of the Sandpiper condominiums—detail. A generously scaled entry walk allows a couple to approach the front door together or guests to gather and pause briefly as they say good night. The atrium-like space was partially open to the sky, allowing for small gardens where exotic plants could thrive in the protected spaces. Walls of glass and sliding doors create a visual blending of interior and exterior spaces, making both seem larger. In addition to planting for visual interest, Krisel directed that these spaces be furnished with interesting elements such as fountain pools and hanging planters.

Gift of William and Corinne Krisel. William Krisel Architectural Archive,
Getty Research Institute, Los Angeles (2009.M.23). © J. Paul Getty Trust.

Twin Palms Landscape
(2011).

Painted by Danny Heller.

NOTES

1. William Krisel, interview with J. C. Miller, June 13, 2015.

2. *1947–1949 USC School of Architecture Course Catalog,* 14. The description for the Landscape Design course (#190 AB&L) read, "The fundamentals of landscape design and its relations to architecture and site planning." The two-semester course was only available to advanced architecture students.

3. Marc Treib and Dorothée Imbert, *Garrett Eckbo: Modern Landscapes for Living* (Berkeley: University of California Press, 1997), 59. Treib has coined the apt term "biocubic" as a descriptor for Eckbo's work, a blend of the smooth-flowing irregular curves of biomorphism and the more angular geometries of analytical Cubism. In interviews later in life, Eckbo acknowledged that he was especially influenced by the work of Wassily Kandinsky, with its sweeping arcs played off against rectangular forms and bold diagonal lines. The work of many of Eckbo's contemporaries, especially those in the San Francisco Bay Area, manifest similar forms.

4. William Krisel, correspondence with J. C. Miller, July 12, 2015.

5. Krisel, interview.

6. Krisel, correspondence with J. C. Miller.

7. Thomas D. Church, *Gardens Are for People* (New York: Reinhold, 1955), 216.

8. Treib and Imbert, *Garrett Eckbo*, 80.

9. Krisel, interview.

10. Ibid.

11. Richard Neutra, *Survival through Design* (New York: Oxford University Press, 1954), 4. In this book, Neutra introduced his "Index of Livability," a conceptual system that allows for evaluation of how well a designed environment responds to the needs of its inhabitants. Examined in light of Neutra's theoretical framework, the integrated environments designed by William Krisel would achieve high scores.

12. Krisel, correspondence with J. C. Miller.

13. Krisel, interview.

This ground-level perspective drawing illustrates Krisel's approach to residential design as a coherent combination of building and site. Dynamic lines in the garden complement the strong geometry of the home. Horizontal and vertical lines in the architecture, fencing, and exterior screen walls calm the composition and contrast nicely with the angled palm trees.

Rendering by William Krisel; graphic illustration by J. C. Miller. Menrad Collection.

the krisel language is still relevant today

CHRIS MENRAD

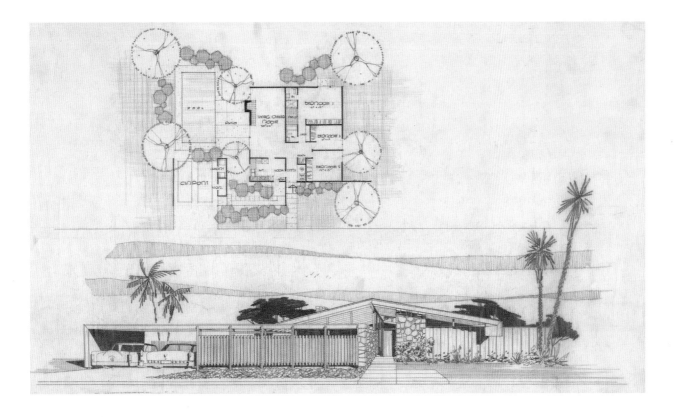

Left: Rendering of a gabled-roof house (Model A-2), Twin Palms, Palm Springs, California (1956)—detail.

Gift of William and Corinne Krisel. William Krisel Architectural Archive, Getty Research Institute, Los Angeles (2009.M.23). © J. Paul Getty Trust.

"What architects do is not a style, it's a way of life. Real architecture has nothing to do with what is 'in' or 'out' of style." — **WILLIAM KRISEL, IN CONVERSATION WITH ALVIN HUANG (2013)**

My story is really the genesis of this book. It is a personal journey that I experienced by living in one of the early homes that William Krisel designed for the Alexander Construction Company, and because of my relationship with William Krisel. My journey began in January 1999. I had spent New Year's Eve in Palm Springs with a friend, and over that short time fell in love with the desert enough to consider buying a house there. Although I had only been to Palm Springs once before, in early 1979, I could see through the faded fabric of the town that there was a special architecture there. Prices were low and I felt that the changing demographics of the baby boom generation would be a source for growth. I had also seen similar places like Miami Beach resurrected through the uniqueness of the local architecture and the feeling of place.

I arrived for my house search not knowing where to find what I was looking for. As I rounded a corner on Palm Canyon, I could see unusual rooflines come into view. They looked to me like the fins of a Cadillac. I headed in their direction and entered a neighborhood that I would soon learn was called Twin Palms. I was awestruck by the originality of the homes—each one was so unique; the area seemed stuck in some kind of time warp, but in a good

Facing: The Dunas Residence, Palm Springs, California (1957)—detail. Joseph Dunas was a partner with the Alexanders in the Twin Palms project. Notice the Cadillac fin–like shape of the roofline.

Photograph by Julius Shulman. Getty Research Institute, Los Angeles (2004.R.10). © J. Paul Getty Trust.

187

way. This was what I wanted. I drove further into the neighborhood and found a house for sale that was being held open. It had the interesting "Cadillac fin" roof. I entered the house and immediately knew this was what I was looking for. On the most basic level, the home was a joy because of its simplicity of plan. It had everything I needed and very little excess.

The house felt like the ultimate expression of what postwar residential architecture in California was all about. It had this leisure aspect, as if it were always vacation time—the soaring ceilings struck me, the view to the palms, mountains, and sky beyond through the clerestory windows, and the tremendous light and openness and ease that I felt there. I loved how the beams that carried the roof expressed the architecture. They made the roof sit lightly on the house, almost as a tent-like structure and so appropriate to the desert environment. I knew nothing of the house's provenance by well-known local builders or of the architectural firm that designed it, but the house felt right to me.

I soon found that the house was known as an "Alexander," referring to the name of the local builder who constructed it. An article just the year before in *The New Yorker* referenced the Alexander name and confirmed what I felt: that I had purchased something good and important.

The design of the homes in the neighborhood was so unique and well done that it took me fully a year to realize that they all had essentially the same floor plan. How ingenious was that? These were all tract homes but they had a particular custom feel about them. I was quite amazed by that. In October 2000, a magazine called *Flaunt* published an article about William Krisel and the Alexander houses. Photographs by noted architectural photographer Julius Shulman taken shortly after the homes were built, both in color and black and white, illustrated the article. I

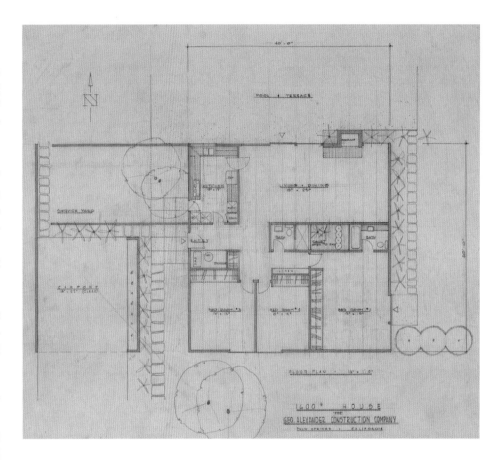

Drawing of an early concept floor plan for a Twin Palms house, Palm Springs, California (circa 1956)—detail. Note that the house plan was 40 by 40 feet, which was very close to what was eventually built.

Rendering of a long-gabled-roof house (Model B-2),
Twin Palms, Palm Springs, California (1956)—detail.

Rendering of a flat-roof house (Model B-3), Twin Palms,
Palm Springs, California (1956)—detail.

Rendering of a sun-flap-roof house (Model A-3),
Twin Palms, Palm Springs, California (1956)—detail.

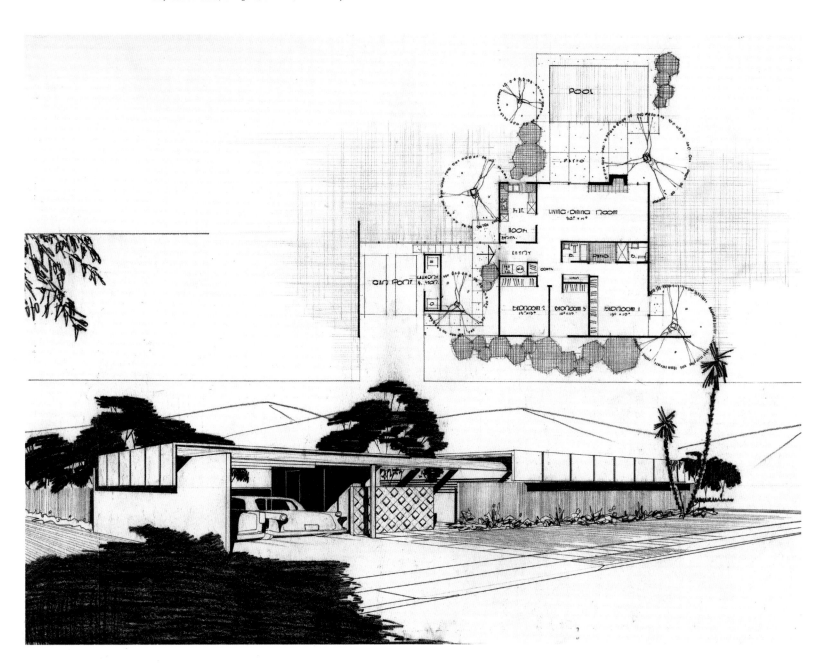

had never seen these, and suddenly the homes came alive for me. I could see that they were very carefully painted, which then fully expressed the architecture that I was feeling in spite of the monochrome paint scheme applied at the time that I purchased my home.

Finally, in 2006, I elected to restore my home. I had seen a lot of renovations that I believed stripped the soul and feeling from these homes. My idea was to do a restoration that would be in the spirit of how the homes were originally presented to the buying public and would help communicate the architect's intent. I wanted to show how these homes really looked and felt when they were new in the hopes that it would influence other renovation work and help preserve the architectural fabric of the city that was slowly becoming an important part of the Palm Springs experience.

Shortly into the project, I contacted the architect, William Krisel. I explained what I was doing and asked for some guidance. I could tell he was frustrated. He told me others had called him before and had not followed his suggestions and advice. He did not offer me much help. A trip to the desert, midway through the renovation, chanced to bring Mr. Krisel to my house. He was quite impressed with the way that I was handling the renovation (I had copied his bathroom cabinets exactly, and worked with his ideas that I saw in the Shulman photographs in *Flaunt*). He decided to help me then and there in any way possible.

He gave me the plans that showed details of how the home was originally designed. He shared with me the original color schemes of the homes. The names and numbers of the paints were from a long-defunct company called Fuller O'Brien. They included descriptive names such as Sea Isle Blue, Cocoa, and Apricot Glow. After much effort, I located

vintage Fuller O'Brien paint chip books on eBay and they revealed to me a very different color palette than I had been made to believe the 1950s represented. As confirmed by the Shulman photographs, the original colors were warm, natural colors that truly reflected the environment of the sky and the mountains, but always anchored by the wonderful Weathered Brown paint color by Dunn-Edwards that all of the wood was painted. Still produced today, the color is a favorite of Krisel's and works so well with the other colors used on stucco and siding. Krisel told me exactly how to paint to achieve his exacting vision and I followed everything he said.

Finally the house was done, with only the front yard landscaping left. Krisel had told me he was a landscape architect and so I asked him if he would design my front yard. He told me he was busy working on a new project, but he would be happy to critique any design I came up with. I created one and forwarded it to him. Within days he returned to me an incredibly complicated but beautiful plan. I had wanted a Zen rock garden, but Krisel, at age eighty-two, created a lyrical masterpiece that to me was like a Mondrian or Kandinsky painting. It spoke to the house and existing palm trees, and integrated both. It was done on a minimal budget utilizing drought-tolerant materials. It was beautiful and unique because it spoke the language of the original era of the house but also worked so well today. I elected to do it, and after working back and forth with Krisel on proportions and plant and ground cover materials, we came up with a plan that I then installed.

The garden created quite a sensation. No one had done anything like it for almost fifty years. I showed my landscape project to a friend of mine, the editorial director of *Metropolis* magazine. It just happened that the magazine was working on an article about restoration of midcentury houses. They

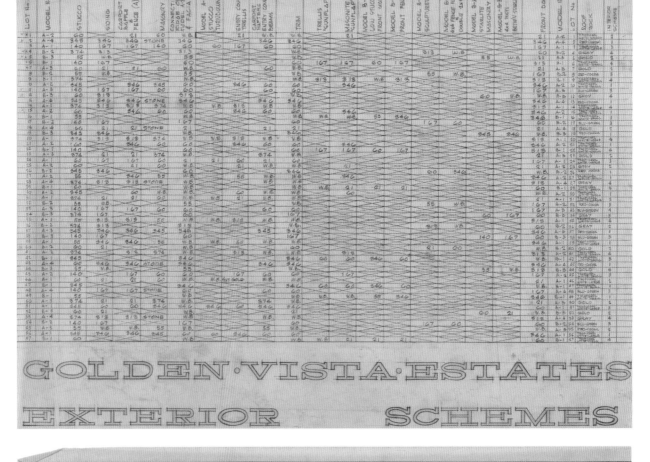

GOLDEN·VISTA·ESTATES
EXTERIOR SCHEMES

GOLDEN·VISTA·ESTATES
INTERIOR SCHEMES

ROOM	DESCRIPTION	SCHEME 1	SCHEME 2	SCHEME 3	SCHEME 4	GENERAL NOTES
LIVING ROOM	WALLS	345	55	140	374	1. NUMBERS FOR PAINT COLORS ARE "O'BRIEN" PAINT CO.
	ACCENT WALL	346	21	167	313	21 - "SUTTERS GOLD" 167 - "SEA-ISLE BLUE"
	FIREPLACE MASONRY WALL	60	60	60	60	55 - "MOONSTONE WHITE" 313 - "APRICOT GLOW"
	FIREPLACE PLASTER HOOD	346	21	167	313	60 - "OFF-WHITE" 345 - "RAFFIA"
	FIREPLACE HEARTH	BLACK	BLACK	BLACK	BLACK	140 - "DAYBREAK" 346 - "COCOA"
	FLOOR - CARPET	OFF-WHITE	OFF-WHITE	OFF-WHITE	OFF-WHITE	374 - "PERSIAN GRAY"
DINING	WALLS	345	55	140	374	
	FLOOR - CARPET	OFF-WHITE	OFF-WHITE	OFF-WHITE	OFF-WHITE	2. RANGE & OVEN ARE "GAFFERS & SATTLER"
KITCHEN	WALLS	345	55	140	374	3. DISHWASHER IS "WASTE KING"
						4. LAMINATED PLASTIC IS "FORMICA"
	RANGE & OVEN	COPPERTONE #1	WHITE	TURQUOISE #5	WHITE	5. VINYL-ASBESTOS FLOORING IS "AMTICO"-CONFETTI ARISTOFLEX
	DISHWASHER	WOOD FRONT	WOOD FRONT	WOOD FRONT	WOOD FRONT	6. CERAMIC TILE KIT COUNTER IS "PACIFIC-TILE"-KRYSTAL-GLAZE-LOW-DECK
	WOOD CABINETS	WHITE-NATURAL	WHITE-NATURAL	WHITE-NATURAL	WHITE-NATURAL	7. SHOWER & TUB WALL TILE IS "GUAMAGRA" BY QUALITY MARBLE & GRANITE
	CERAMIC TILE	57	52	53	58	8. SHOWER FLOOR & DAM TILE IS "PACIFIC-TILE"-KRYSTAL-GLAZE
	FORMICA FOOD BAR	F-949	F-949	F-949	F-949	9. ALL CEILINGS (EXCEPT FURRED C'LGS) ARE CELOTEX
	FLOOR VINYL ASBESTOS	774	768	766	753	10. ALL WOOD BEAMS TO BE PAINTED "DURO EDWARDS WEATHERED BROWN"
BATH Nº1	WALLS	345	55	140	374	11. ENTRY HALL FLOOR IS "AMTICO" RENAISSANCE - 12"x12" #1
	CEILING	60	60	60	60	12. ENTRY HALL "SHOJI" WALLPAPER IS "WINFIELD"
	FLOOR	774	768	766	753	13. ALL PLUMBING IS AMERICAN STANDARD-WHITE EXCEPT BATHRM
	CER. TILE WALLS	BEIGE-MEDLEY	BLACK-GRAY-RED MEDLEY	BLUE-MEDLEY	BLACK-GRAY-RED MEDLEY	14. ALL CARPET NUMBERS AS PER "PERRY GILL" DESIGNATION
	CER. TILE FLOOR & DAM	57	52	53	58	
	MARBLE	ALAMASCADO (TAN)	GRIS-PEARL (GRAY)	CALACATA (WHITE)	GRIS-PEARL (GRAY)	
	PULLMAN VALENCE	346	21	167	313	
	BATH FIXTURES	PERSIAN BROWN	PLATINUM GRAY	REGENCY BLUE	PLATINUM GRAY	
	FLOOR - VINYL ASBESTOS	774	768	766	753	
BATH Nº2	WALLS	345	55	140	374	
	CEILING	60	60	60	60	
	SHELF APRON & LITE VALENCE	346	21	167	313	
	CER. TILE AROUND TUB	BEIGE-MEDLEY	BLACK-GRAY-RED MEDLEY	BLUE-MEDLEY	BLACK-GRAY-RED MEDLEY	
	CORALITE SLIDING PANELS	WHITE	WHITE	WHITE	WHITE	
	FORMICA CABINET FRAME	879 BEIGE	893 PRIMROSE	921 AQUA	F-872 PUMPKIN	
	FLOOR - VINYL ASBESTOS	774	768	766	753	
ENTRY & HALL	WALLS	345	55	140	374	
	CEILING (PLASTER)	60	60	60	60	
	"SHOJI DOORS" PAPER	2902-SANDSTONE	2534-MEDICI GOLD	2532-CAPRI	2501-TAJ-WHITE	

View from the front yard of the Alexanders' Twin Palms house, with the Dunas Residence (left) and model homes with various exterior paint colors (1957).

Interior of the Alexander
Residence, Twin Palms,
Palm Springs, California,
designed by William
Krisel (1957).

Original kitchen with simple construction using
pegboard and maple wood (1957).

Sun-flap-roof house (Model A-3) before restoration,
Twin Palms, Palm Springs, California (circa 2005).

Newly restored gable-roof house (Model A-2), with
Krisel-designed landscaping and original exterior colors (2012).

Photograph © Darren Bradley.

New version of a Krisel kitchen (2011).

Photograph © Darren Bradley.

had an East Coast example, a Florida example, and were looking for something on the West Coast. My project (specifically the landscape) was included in an August 2006 article in the magazine. Within days of publication, Krisel reported to me that he was getting calls and reconnecting with people he hadn't heard from in years, congratulating him on the work. The article was the beginning of a new recognition of him and his work. It was more than I could have asked for. The house and garden were soon nominated as a Class One Historic Site, and I started to see the influence of the work in other restoration projects throughout the city.

But what was that project Krisel was working on when I asked about the landscape? A year before, a Canadian builder had stayed at my home (then also a vacation rental) and was so intrigued by the design and its elegance in construction that when I told him my home was not for sale, he contacted William Krisel. They were working together to create the first new examples of Krisel's now famous butterfly-roof house for a new homebuyer. It was a challenge to bring the design up to current codes and have the house still look as it had originally, but to date, six of these "new" Krisels stand in Palm Springs. The new homes may be one of the only examples where a living architect has recreated a fifty-year-old design.

Subsequently, a friend of mine, J. R. Roberts, and I worked together to restore two other Krisel/Alexander homes with the advice and input of Krisel, working with his design language. Each has the exact look and feel it originally had, but still works with today's way of living. Unique landscaping was created for these homes, again by Krisel, working with existing concrete and plant material and on a budget. I learned that he excelled at solving problems when budget was a consideration. It is why he was so successful in

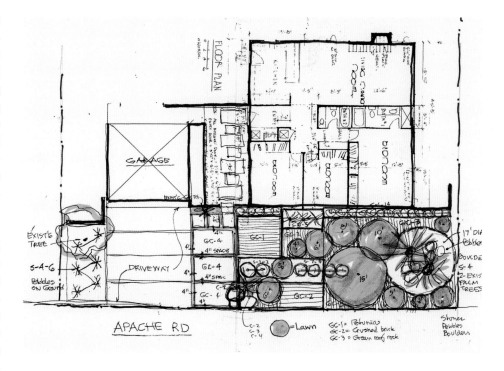

Menrad Residence garden plan (2006).

Menrad Collection.

working with developers. He knew how to help them make money without sacrificing good design. Of the four restored Krisel homes, including my own, two have received a Class One Historic Site designation for their architecture and one is pending.

It has been almost ten years now since my house was renovated. It still looks the same—as fresh as when it was first built. The landscaping and renovations have had their influence and a whole new group of people have become interested in these important homes. I have forged a deep relationship with William Krisel and his lovely wife, Corinne, over all these years and projects, and I consider myself lucky to have learned and worked with this remarkable artist.

Above: A newly created kitchen
inspired by William Krisel's design
brings an authentic feeling to a
freshly renovated Alexander home
(2012).

Photograph by Henry Connell.

Left: A new version of the famous
butterfly-roof house, Palm Springs,
California (2009).

Photograph © Darren Bradley.

Interior view of the Buzyn Residence,
Palm Springs, California (2015).

Photograph © Darren Bradley.

204

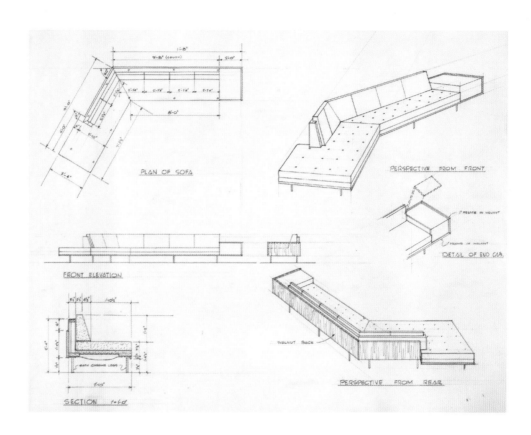

Above: Drawing for a built-in sofa and
side table (circa 1957).

Left: Interior view of a Twin Palms tract house,
Palm Springs, California, with Krisel-designed
built-in sofa and side table (circa 1957).

Below: Exterior detail of a restored Twin Palms tract house, Palm Springs, California (2015).

Facing: Exterior view of a restored Racquet Club Road Estates house, Palm Springs, California (2015).

Photographs © Darren Bradley.

WILLIAM KRISEL

A.I.A.

ARCHITECT

william krisel, an everyday modernist

JAKE GORST

"Bill devoted his complete life to his architecture, but at the same time he had a huge interest, and a passionate interest, about the world around him. He was lucky to have the children and I who understood and stood by him."

—CORINNE KRISEL

Facing: Detail of William Krisel office sign (2015).

Photograph by Chris Menrad. Menrad Collection.

Left: William, Michelle, Corinne, and Billy Krisel (left to right) in their Tigertail Road home designed by Krisel, Brentwood, California (circa 1957).

Collection of William and Corinne Krisel.

Middle: William Krisel (circa 1954).

Collection of William and Corinne Krisel.

Right: Movie poster and DVD cover for the documentary film *William Krisel, Architect* (2010).

Collection of Jake and Tracey Gorst.

Corinne Krisel knew exactly what William Krisel was all about before she married him. "I knew that architecture was his whole life," she told friend Jim West and me one afternoon in the Krisel's family home in Brentwood in February 2009. "That was his number one priority in life—and I wasn't going to be number one. Architecture was going to be number one."[1]

Bill was sitting beside her with a big smile on his face. It was obvious to me that they loved each other very much. Corinne continued to describe their life together with great candor: "We have always had a family life that was close and rich, but we all got out of his way because Bill had to be Bill. My pride and love for Bill was always how committed, conscientious, and caring he was for his profession—how he never compromised in any way. On every project, no matter how small it was (it could have been very little—maybe an add-on), he gave the same commitment, the same conscientiousness, the same devotion that he would to a project that was quite large. Bill devoted his complete life to his architecture, but at the same time he had a huge interest, and a passionate interest, about the world around him. He was lucky to have the children and I who understood and stood by him."[2]

The Krisel children understood that their home life was different than most, and they developed a life philosophy that shaped their approach as they moved into adulthood.

"Bill honed his design and construction techniques into the Modern aesthetic we now love." — LEO MARMOL

Daughter Michelle explained, "As hard as my dad worked, he managed to be home every single night at 6 p.m. to have dinner with us. And when I say 6 p.m., I don't mean 6:03 or 6:05. I mean 6 p.m.—and dinner and everything had to be ready precisely at that time. And I think that was fantastic with everything that he was juggling to make it a priority that we had dinner every night. But it was those dinner conversations, which were exclusively about him and his work until my mom sort of interjected with what Billy and Missy had actually done that day at school, that were the model for the life I lead—which is that you love what you do, but you don't do it just because you love it. You do it really well. You accomplish something. You do good for other people. And *that* is a life worth living."[3]

Bill knew that his work was important. Many World War II veterans returned to the States, got married, and had families, and there was a tremendous postwar need for housing. There was also a great need for the commercial structures that supported these vast, growing communities. Most of the people living in the more than thirty thousand residential housing units that Bill designed had no idea who he was. But their lives were enriched through his imagination and creativity. He devoted his time and energy throughout the decades to provide for the needs of hundreds of thousands of strangers, and it was a joy to him. "I really didn't think I was doing anything other than what I liked to do," he said.[4]

In the early 1990s, the architecture projects waned. Bill turned to other endeavors, including serving as an expert architecture witness providing testimony at court proceedings. It was a new chapter in his life—a quieter one. He was satisfied with it. But people with an interest in Midcentury Modern design were beginning to rediscover Bill's earlier work, including the 1950s California homes he designed for the Alexander Construction Company in Palm Springs, and the Sandpiper condominiums in Palm Desert. They recognized how culturally significant the structures were, and started reaching out to him, asking questions. He had saved practically every drawing he had ever produced over the course of his life—thousands of renderings, working drawings, and other papers. With these inquiries he started to revisit his archive. He had no idea of the level of recognition that he was about to receive.

In 2001, the Palm Springs Preservation Foundation hosted the Great Alexander Weekend, an event celebrating the tract house work of the Alexander Construction Company and architects Bill Krisel and Donald Wexler. Writer Alan Hess produced the book *Palm Springs Weekend,* featuring Bill's work. Since then, Hess has also produced the books *Julius Shulman: Palm Springs* and *The Ranch House,* both featuring Bill Krisel. He was also featured in the book *The Desert Modernists: The Architects Who Envisioned Midcentury Modern Palm Springs,* published by Modernism Week in 2015.

In 2004, I was asked to direct the documentary film *Desert Utopia: Midcentury Architecture in Palm Springs,* which contained a ten-minute segment about Bill. The Denver-based organization Design Onscreen, under the direction of H. Kirk Brown III and Jill A. Wiltse, asked me to produce a ninety-minute feature film about Bill, *William Krisel, Architect,* five years later. The premiere of the film took place on February 14, 2010, to a sold-out crowd at the Camelot Theatres in Palm Springs. Bill and Corinne were the guests of honor. Following the screening, Bill participated in a lengthy question-and-answer session. A similar event took place at the Harold M. Williams Auditorium at the Getty Center in Los Angeles one month later.

In 2009, architect Zoltan Pali, in conjunction with the Museum of Design Art and Architecture in Culver City, California, curated The Architecture of William Krisel, AIA, an exhibition featuring many of Bill's photographs and drawings. The exhibition traveled to Palm Springs and Denver, Colorado. Shortly afterwards, the Getty Research Institute accepted Bill's vast collection of papers, including drawings and correspondence, into its permanent inventory. Thus his name was added to an exclusive list of progressive Southern Californian architects whose work is also held by the institute, including Pierre Koenig, John Lautner, Ray Kappe, and Frank Israel.

On February 13, 2009, Bill was also honored with a star on the Palm Springs Walk of Stars. At the sidewalk dedication ceremony that morning, master of ceremonies Michael Stern, an artist and historian, said, "A critical ingredient in the Modernist ideal is that architecture should influence and enlighten the human spirit. . . . Something that can influence life on a general level—to create an architecture of joy, but at an affordable price. A Modernism for the masses. Today we are honoring someone who has fulfilled that challenging goal with style and true architecture—the kind that begins with a capital 'A.' Bill is a virtuoso at creating so much from so little—and it is a testament to his caliber that he didn't create mundane tracts that are based on numbing, endless, banal repetition, but instead created true neighborhoods that *feel* like neighborhoods oozing with vitality and charm."[5]

Stern went on to discuss the efforts that were being made to restore many of the Krisel-designed Alexander homes throughout Palm Springs to their original condition. Loving efforts to do the same have continued with Krisel homes in Northridge, Los Angeles, San Diego, Las Vegas, and elsewhere. Even new homes have been built according to Bill's specifications.

Architect Leo Marmol said in a recent interview, "As an architect, Bill's fluency in construction allowed him to optimize every architectural detail. Bill honed his design and construction techniques into the Modern aesthetic we now love. Bill gracefully bridged the divide between the architect and the builder to create a

William Krisel is honored with a star on the Palm Springs Walk of Stars, Palm Springs, California (February 13, 2009).

Collection of Jake and Tracey Gorst.

timeless and modern sense of residential comfort. The recent recognition of Bill's work via celebrations and retrospectives is long overdue. However, it is the increased interest in restoring Bill's houses that I find to be the most long-lasting and significant recognition."[6]

Architectural historian John Crosse mirrored these sentiments. "These are really his glory years. All of this preservation going on—it just brings more and more recognition to his work and people are starting to see not only are these tracts part of his body of work, there's so much more out there in terms of commercial development, high rises, office buildings, condominiums. . . . He's the Modernist for everyday life for a whole era of Southern California development."[7]

Sadly, in 2014, Bill and Corinne's longtime residence in Brentwood—a masterpiece designed by Bill in 1955—was demolished after a series of unfortunate real estate transactions. Not only was it heartbreaking to the Krisel family and friends, but the uproar in the press and the reaction from the public was significant. This was further evidence of a notable shift in the way architecture is being reported on in recent years. "The old guard that focused on a few well known high art architects is passing," said Alan Hess. "A new generation of historians are reassessing things with new research."[8]

There is a movement to document the work of twentieth-century architects who worked hard and touched the lives of large populations, but who had little desire for fame. This history is being recounted with a human touch, and is appealing to people who perhaps have had little or no previous interest in architecture or design. Bill's architecture, his personal story, his hard work ethic, his diligent efforts to preserve and protect his own archive, and his willingness to share his experiences with others have contributed to this shift in public awareness.

I really enjoyed that February morning with the Krisels in 2009. They were so open, telling many interesting stories. Reflecting on their life together towards the end of the visit, Corinne smiled and said, "We sure packed a lot in our lives. We've just felt that we never missed out on anything. We really fit it all in. And when Bill just stayed with his commitment, his beliefs, of good work for the masses, everybody else didn't get all excited about it. It didn't matter. Look at the nice reward everybody is getting."[9]

NOTES

1. Corrine Krisel, in discussion with Jake Gorst, February 2009.

2. Ibid.

3. Michelle Krisel, in discussion with Jake Gorst, May 2009.

4. William Krisel, in discussion with Jake Gorst, February 2009.

5. Michael Stern, from a recording made by Jake Gorst of Stern's address at the Walk of Stars dedication, February 13, 2009.

6. Leo Marmol, in discussion with Jake Gorst, July 2015.

7. John Crosse, in discussion with Jake Gorst, March 2009.

8. Alan Hess, in discussion with Jake Gorst, July 2015.

9. Corrine Krisel, in discussion with Jake Gorst.

bibliography

BETHANY MORSE

Atwell, Jeff. "Alexander Unwrapped." *At Home Magazine,* May 2004, 18–25.

Biller, Steven. "Zen and the Art of Modernism." *At Home Magazine,* November 2002, 12–20.

"Bold Geometric Design Is a Striking Foil to Its Desert Setting." *House and Home,* August 1962, 83.

Bradley, Darren. "William Krisel." *Modernist Architecture* (blog), June 29, 2013. modernistarchitecture.blogspot.com/2013/06/william-krisel.html.

"The Challenge—A Tract House: Luxury Look on a Budget." *Los Angeles Times,* April 12, 1959, Home section, J30–J31.

Chang, Jade. "Paying Proper Homage." *Metropolis,* January 2006, 90–91.

"Co-Op Living: The New Trend in the Desert." *Palm Springs Life,* December 1960, 11–17.

Coquelle, Aline. *Palm Springs Style.* Translated by Sharon Grevet. New York: Assouline, 2005.

Crosse, John. "William Krisel: Annotated Bibliography." Unpublished manuscript, last modified 2008.

———. *William Krisel Oral History.* Playa del Rey, CA: modern-ISM Press, 2009.

———. "William Krisel and George Alexander in Hollywood, 1937–1956." *Southern California Architectural History* (blog), January 13, 2011. socalarchhistory.blogspot.com/2011/01/william-krisel-and-george-alexanders.html.

Culver, Lawrence. *The Frontier of Leisure: Southern California and the Shaping of Modern America.* New York: Oxford University Press, 2010.

de Wit, Wim, and Christopher James Alexander, eds. *Overdrive: L.A. Constructs the Future, 1940–1990.* Los Angeles: Getty Research Institute, 2013.

Desert Utopia: Midcentury Architecture in Palm Springs. DVD. Produced by Jill A. Wiltse, H. Kirk Brown III, and David Shearer. Directed by Jake Gorst. Denver, CO: Design Onscreen, 2004.

Edmundson, Joshua. "Development in Southern California after World War II: Architecture, Photography, & Design." *History in the Making* 7 (2014): 125–46, historyinthemaking.csusb.edu/documents/HistoryintheMaking2014finalprint_000.pdf#page=141.

Engel, Allison. "A Lesson in Long-Lasting Design." *Palm Desert Magazine,* Winter 2006, 54–59.

———. "Modern Love." *Palm Springs Life,* February 2007, 86–97.

"Famed Architect's Achievements Recognized by Modern Design Group." *Riverside Press-Enterprise,* October 17, 2006, B3.

Fong, Dominique. "Purist works with famed architect to restore Palm Springs midcentury homes." *Desert Sun,* February 19, 2014. archive.desertsun.com/article/20140219/LIFESTYLES1101/302190022/Chris-Menrad-works-with-famed-architect-restore-Palm-Springs-midcentury-homes.

"Four Awards Won by Firm." *Los Angeles Times,* January 26, 1958, F6.

Grasso, Gary. "Open House: Palm Springs." *Atomic Ranch,* Summer 2009, 74–79.

"Group of 66 Air-Conditioned Speculative Builder Houses, Smoke Tree Valley Estates, Palm Springs; Architects: Palmer & Krisel." *Progressive Architecture,* March 1958, 146–49.

Harlan, James. *The Alexanders: A Desert Legacy.* Palm Springs, CA: Palm Springs Preservation Foundation, 2011.

———. "Standing the Test of Time: The Palm Springs Alexanders." *Modernism Magazine,* March 2011, 76–77.

Harris, Chloe. "Desert Cool." *California Home + Design,* May 2008, 102–09.

Hess, Alan. *The Ranch House.* New York: Abrams, 2005.

———. *Forgotten Modern: California Houses 1940–1970.* Layton, UT: Gibbs Smith, 2007.

Hess, Alan, and Andrew Danish. *Palm Springs Weekend: The Architecture and Design of a Midcentury Oasis.* San Francisco: Chronicle, 2001.

Heumann, Leslie, Teresa Grimes, and Peter Moruzzi. "City of Rancho Mirage Historic Resources Survey." Rancho Mirage, CA: City of Rancho Mirage, 2003. www.ranchomirageca.gov/content_files/pdf/city_government/city_commissions/historic_preservation/final_report.pdf.

Howell-Ardila, Deborah. "Writing our own program: the USC experiment in modern architectural pedagogy, 1930 to 1960." MHP thesis, University of Southern California, 2010. digitallibrary.usc.edu/cdm/ref/collection/p15799coll127/id/414079.

Karol, Lawrence. "Quiet—and Idyllic—on the Set!" *Palm Springs Life,* July 2013. www.palmspringslife.com/Palm-Springs-Life/July-2013/Quiet-and-Idyllic-on-the-Set.

Krisel, William, and Wim de Wit. *Conversation with William Krisel Regarding the Film* William Krisel, Architect. DVD. Recorded April 13, 2010. Los Angeles: Getty Research Institute Public Event Recordings, 2002– (IA40002).

"Letters." *Time,* November 14, 1938. www.time.com/time/magazine/article/0,9171,771997,00.html.

Levine, Bettijane. "Modern's Everyman." *Los Angeles Times,* February 14, 2008. articles.latimes.com/2008/feb/14/home/hm-krisel14.

McCoy, Esther. "What I Believe: A Statement of Palmer and Krisel's Architectural Principles." *Los Angeles Times,* May 20, 1956: Q4–5, Q29.

Mid-Century Moderns: The Homes That Define Palm Springs. DVD. Produced by John C. Brown and Bert Simonis. Directed by John C. Brown. Sonora, CA: This 'n That Films, 2013.

Morrow, Greg. "Woodland Hills/Canoga Park." Chap. 7.2 in "The Homeowner Revolution: Democracy, Land Use and the Los Angeles Slow-Growth Movement, 1965–1992." PhD diss., University of California Los Angeles, 2013. escholarship.org/uc/item/6k64g20f.

Muzio, Louise. "William Krisel—Visionary Architect." Better Living Socal, July 26, 2014. betterlivingsocal.com/william-krisel-visionary-architect.

Newman, Morris. "Masters of Modernism—The Butterfly Effect." *Palm Springs Life,* February 2009. www.palmspringslife.com/palm-springs-life/february-2009/masters-of-modernism-the-butterfly-effect.

Niemann, Greg. *Palm Springs Legends: Creation of a Desert Oasis.* San Diego: Sunbelt, 2006.

"Ocotillo Lodge." *Concrete Masonry Age,* January 1959, 12–15.

O'Kelly, Emma. "Desert Bloomer." *Wallpaper,* May 2012, 252–59.

Penn, Jean. "The New Alexanders." *Palm Springs Life,* November 2000, 68–72.

Rippingale, Sally Presley. *The History of the Racquet Club of Palm Springs.* Yucaipa, CA: US Business Specialities, 1985.

Rovito, Lisa Marie. "Old House, New House." *Palm Springs Life,* April 2007, 128–34.

"Roy Fey's Canyon Estates: Luxurious Homes and Condominium Living." *Palm Springs Life,* November 1969, 25–28.

"Sandpiper." *Concrete Masonry Age,* January 1959, 6–11.

Schnepf, James, Karen Prinzmetal, Jim West, Jeff Yeager, Sharie Yeager, and the Historical Society of Palm Desert. *Sandpiper Palm Desert, 1958–1969.* Palm Springs, CA: Modernism Week, 2013.

"Speculative Builder Houses: Palm Springs, California." *Progressive Architecture,* March 1958, 146–49.

Stern, Michael, and Alan Hess. *Julius Shulman: Palm Springs.* New York: Rizzoli, 2008. Published in conjunction with the exhibition of the same name, shown at the Palm Springs Art Museum, February 15 through May 4, 2008.

Stern, Michael, Julius Shulman, Alan Hess, David Martin, and Palm Springs Art Museum. Julius Shulman: Desert Modern. Palm Springs, CA: Palm Springs Art Museum, 2008.

Visions of Utopia: Three Architects Conference. DVD. Produced by H. Kirk Brown III, Jill A. Wiltse, Jake Gorst, Tracey Rennie Gorst, Robert Imber, and David Shearer. Directed by David Shearer. Northport, NY: Mainspring Pictures, 2015.

Weiner, Stewart, ed. *The Desert Modernists: The Architects Who Envisioned Midcentury Modern Palm Springs.* Palm Springs, CA: Modernism Week, 2015.

Weinstein, Dave. "Krisel Face to Face." *CA Modern,* Summer 2006, 16–17.

West, Jim. *William Krisel, A.I.A.: Architect and Landscape Architect.* Palm Desert, CA: privately printed, 2006.

When Mod Went Mass: A Celebration of Alexander Homes. Palm Springs, CA: Palm Springs Historic Site Foundation, 2001.

William Krisel, Architect. DVD (2 disks). Produced by Jill A. Wiltse, H. Kirk Brown III, and Heather Purcell. Directed by Jake Gorst. Denver, CO: Design Onscreen, 2010.

William Krisel papers, 1935–2014. Collection Number 2009.M.23. Los Angeles: Getty Research Institute, Special Collections.

Winship, Sian. *Exiles and Emigres in Los Angeles Modernist Architecture.* Sherman Oaks, CA: Society of Architectural Historians/Southern California Chapter, 1997.

———. "Quantity and quality: architects working for developers in southern California, 1960–1973." Master's thesis, University of Southern California, 2011.cdm15799.contentdm.oclc.org/cdm/ref/collection/p15799coll127/id/657553.

"The Wonderful World of Canyon View Estates." *Palm Springs Life,* November 1965.

list of contributors

Darren Bradley is an award-winning architectural photographer with a love of Modernism and the built environment. His work has appeared in art books, journals, and lifestyle magazines around the world. His awards include the 2013 Paris Prix de la Photographie for the Advertising-Architecture category. He lives in a Krisel-designed home in San Diego.

Heidi Creighton is a researcher and writer. She divides her time between Palm Springs and Vancouver, British Columbia.

Wim de Wit is an adjunct curator of architecture and design at the Cantor Arts Center at Stanford University. He studied architectural history at the Catholic University in Nijmegen, the Netherlands. His field of expertise is the history of Modern architecture in Europe and the United States. After graduation, he was appointed as a scholarly researcher at the Netherlands Documentation Center for Architecture in Amsterdam. He moved to the United States in 1982 and first worked as a guest curator at the Cooper Hewitt Museum in New York. From 1983 until 1993 he was the curator for architecture at the Chicago Historical Society, and from 1993 to 2013 he was the head of Special Collections and later of the Department of Architecture and Contemporary Art at the Getty Research Institute in Los Angeles. He was president of the board of the International Confederation of Architectural Museums between 1994 and 1998, and was a member of the board of the Society of Architectural Historians from 1988 to 1991, and from 2009 to 2012.

Jake Gorst is the author of the book *Andrew Geller: Deconstructed* (Glitterati, 2015). He is also an Emmy award–winning documentary filmmaker and the director of Mainspring Pictures Ltd. Recent films he's directed include *The Nature of Modernism: E. Stewart Williams, Architect* (Design Onscreen, 2014), *Modern Tide: Midcentury Architecture on Long Island* (Design Onscreen, 2012), *William Krisel, Architect* (Design Onscreen, 2010), *Journeyman Architect: The Life and Work of Donald Wexler* (Design Onscreen, 2009), and *Desert Utopia: Midcentury Architecture in Palm Springs* (Design Onscreen, 2006).

Jim Harlan is a residential architect who splits his time between Palm Springs and Pasadena, California.

Alan Hess, an architect and historian, has authored nineteen books on Modern architecture and urbanism in the mid-twentieth century, including books on John Lautner, Oscar Niemeyer, Frank Lloyd Wright, the ranch house, Googie architecture, Las Vegas, and Palm Springs. He is the architecture critic of the *San Jose Mercury News,* a contributor to *The Architect's Newspaper,* a Graham Foundation grant recipient, and a National Arts Journalism Program Fellow. He has received the Honor Award from the National Trust for Historic Preservation, and the President's Award from the Los Angeles Conservancy for three decades of work in preserving Modern architecture.

Barbara Lamprecht earned her M.Arch. at Cal Poly Pomona and her Ph.D. at the University of Liverpool. Her dissertation was on Richard Neutra's architectural approach that considers the body, senses, and perception as related to the natural environment. Dr. Lamprecht writes National Register of Historic Places nominations, evaluates properties, and acts as a project manager on rehabilitating buildings. She was the historical consultant to the Roman Catholic Diocese of Orange on the award-winning rehabilitation of Neutra's famous Garden Grove church campus. She has co-curated two exhibitions, both focused on little-known but excellent examples of Modernism in Bakersfield, California. She has written for publications including *The Architectural Review* and *Harvard Design Magazine,* and is the author of three books on Neutra, including his catalogue raisonné (Taschen, 2000) and *Richard Neutra: Furniture: The Body and Senses* (Wasmuth, 2015).

Chris Menrad is an enthusiast for all things midcentury, from cars to art to architecture. After working on Wall Street as a stock trader he let his love of modern design lure him to Palm Springs, where he became a founding member of the Palm Springs Modern Committee, a nonprofit preservation organization, of which he is currently its president. He is active in Palm Springs real estate as a local agent representing both buyers and sellers of midcentury homes, and has restored several midcentury homes in the Palm Springs area.

J. C. Miller is a licensed landscape architect and writer with a deep interest in history and the ethical frameworks that guide the creation of the built environment. He has a certificate in landscape architecture from the University of California Berkeley. He is currently a partner at Vallier Design Associates, a landscape architecture and planning practice located in the San Francisco Bay Area, and the former director for the Certificate Program in Landscape Architecture at UC Berkeley Extension. Mr. Miller is a coauthor of *Modern Public Gardens: Robert Royston and the Suburban Park,* an examination of the innovative postwar park and playgrounds designed by Robert Royston.

Bethany Morse earned her master of arts in architectural history from the University of Texas at Austin in 2013. Primarily focused on Modern architecture and architects, she often looks at the subject through an interdisciplinary or cultural lens. She is currently working on publishing her first article about the inspiration for Richard Neutra's theory of biorealism.

Jim West and his wife Karen Prinzmetal are preservationists who happily live and wander daily between their two Krisel-designed Sandpiper homes located in Palm Desert, California. One home was built in 1959 and the other in 1963. Their somewhat eccentric life is filled with art, architectural design, and charity.

Sian Winship is an architectural historian, writer, and fourth-generation native Californian. As a board member of the Society of Architectural Historians/Southern California Chapter for twenty years, she has curated many local and national tours of Modern architecture, including *Exiles and Emigres in Los Angeles Modern Architecture* and *Out of the Shadow: Phoenix Modernism After Frank Lloyd Wright.* In 2011, she earned her master of historic preservation degree from the USC School of Architecture.

index

Film still from the documentary
film *William Krisel, Architect,*
directed by Jake Gorst (2010).

Collection of Jake and Tracey Gorst.